SUCCESS JOURNAL

**A PRODUCTIVITY
GOAL PLANNER**

ROCK
POINT

Matthias Hechler

Brimming with creative inspiration, how-to projects, and useful information to enrich your everyday life, Quarto Knows is a favorite destination for those pursuing their interests and passions. Visit our site and dig deeper with our books into your area of interest: Quarto Creates, Quarto Cooks, Quarto Homes, Quarto Lives, Quarto Drives, Quarto Explores, Quarto Gifts, or Quarto Kids.

Inspiring | Educating | Creating | Entertaining

Published in 2019 by Rock Point,
an imprint of The Quarto Group
142 West 36th Street, 4th Floor
New York, NY 10018, USA
T (212) 779-4972 F (212) 779-6058
www.QuartoKnows.com

First published in Germany under the title *Dranbleiben Erfolgsjournal* by DRANBLEIBEN Journaling Tools in 2018.

Rock Point titles are also available at discount for retail, wholesale, promotional, and bulk purchase. For details, contact the Special Sales Manager by email at specialsales@quarto.com or by mail at The Quarto Group, Attn: Special Sales Manager, 100 Cummings Center Suite 265D, Beverly, MA 01915 USA.

10 9 8 7 6 5 4 3 2 1

ISBN: 978-1-63106-664-1

English translation by Julia Scales

Editorial Director: Rage Kindelsperger
Creative Director: Laura Drew
Managing Editor: Cara Donaldson
Senior Editor: John Foster
Cover and Interior Design: IXTENSA GmbH & Co. KG

Printed in China

A Gift for Your Life

The *Success Journal* has been created for anyone who wants to live a more constructive, successful, structured, focused, and fulfilling life. This is a powerful instrument to permanently establish new routines, habits, and rituals in your life that are not only good for you but also help you achieve your goals.

You will find it to be a faithful traveling companion and tireless training partner on the path to your goals, ambitions, and visions and it will help you stay on track for **100 days**—because that's how long it takes to see a real change in your life.

Consider this journal the secret to transforming your life!

This journal belongs to:

LESLIE

Period:

From: 3/7/21   To:

GET STARTED
—
TODAY!

MY SUGGESTIONS FOR GETTING STARTED:

Read the introduction up to page 47 but *do not* fill out anything at first.

Identify a small goal that you can easily achieve in two to four weeks. Write it down on page 44 and add a visualization on page 48.

TIP: A good goal can simply be defining your overall life vision with a few starting goals!

Get started with the first journaling section on page 52 and keep writing, because maintaining momentum is the most important thing.

The *Success Journal* will give you everything else you'll need on your journey. You will define your vision, core values, fundamental principles, further goals, visualizations, a "wheel of life," and personal power questions. You will also discover some self-critical beliefs and replace them with positive ones. All you need to do is write everything down on the following pages where prompted (as well as in the Notes sections, if you run out of room).

> "
>
> My suggestions should not be taken as strict dogma, but rather as reflections from my own experiences. Like many people, I like to see quick results, which is why I recommend you begin to journal with one small, simple goal. Or, if you prefer, work through this introduction before you start journaling—choose whichever way best works for you.

Contents

How This Journal Began

A few years ago, I couldn't get out of bed on most mornings.
I had no motivation . . . and zero energy. I didn't want to get up;
in fact, I *couldn't* get up. The duvet cover lying on top of me felt
like it was made of lead. An existential crisis had grabbed me
firmly by the neck with its mighty hand. How did this happen?

Somehow, I had seen it coming, but the feeling of being torn apart and paralyzed
was frightening. Was I burned out? "I can't complain," I told myself, which is
something we always say to ourselves when we think we should be feeling good.
I had been an entrepreneur for many years, had made enough money for a good
life, lived with my children in our own house, and had just overcome a difficult
personal situation.

Nevertheless, I entered a phase of fear, self-doubt, inconceivable futility, and
paralyzing powerlessness. I would ask myself, "Who am I? What can I really offer?
Where am I supposed to get the strength to handle this? How am I supposed to
shoulder all of the responsibility that rests on me?" I felt like a child in need of
protection; I was scared and overwhelmed. I would have loved to hide under my
heavy duvet forever.

But I had to get up.

Staying in bed and giving up wasn't an option for me. If nothing else, I knew my
children needed me to be a fit, strong, and alert dad. I had to pull myself up by
my bootstraps and get it together. I knew I had to heighten my self-awareness
and keep a clear mind to pull myself out of this mental fog. Looking back, my life
during that time felt like I was clinging onto an anchored buoy after an exhausting, aimless trip in a small fishing boat on a rough, high sea.

Before this difficult time, during my early twenties, I was always interested
in positive thinking and helpful self-affirmations. I remembered reading
Subconscious Mind: A Source of Unlimited Power by Erhard Freitag and feeling

inspired by what the author promised. The idea that all I had to do was think and believe intensely enough in a certain direction to achieve a goal was like the promise of paradise for me, even better than money or success.

I read countless self-help books, including some by author Joseph Murphy and attend seminars, and soon experienced amazing successes that made me believe in the power of our minds. I knew self-help and motivation techniques were not just some esoteric hocus-pocus nonsense.

With motivational thinking, I would put myself in a good place, but just as quickly as success came into my life, it quickly disappeared. What began as an almost limitless euphoria would slowly ebb away, little by little, down the drain and would soon vanish. It was washed away by everyday life, dwindling focus, distractions of love, and the exhausting years of starting my own business. I didn't notice at first, but when I did come up for air, my focus was gone, and I was left feeling alone and confused.

It wasn't until a few years later that I re-encountered the power of positive thinking, but this time in a business-related context. Revisiting the motivational-thinking topics rekindled a fire in me, and the power of a positive mindset and personality resonated with me again. Success followed soon after, until— once again—it all vanished into thin air. It was a slow process, and it wasn't until several months later that it hit me: most of the positive things in my life were gone. How could that be? It was frustrating and somewhat depressing, considering what I had believed was a continuing fire that would keep burning was, instead, only a flash in the pan.

Although I practiced the power of positivity, it seemed I always ended up in the same grind. I felt inadequate and often doubted myself. I began to accept this recurring slump as my fate. I would tell myself, "This is how life is. This is who I am. I'm just not good and consistent enough to get it right."

Does this scenario sound familiar?

I continued this negative self-talk and repeated the self-critical cycle several times until a few years ago. Then, I decided to go back to square one: I read more books, worked with motivational techniques, and practiced visualizations. I realized that I hadn't been doing anything positive for months and was stuck in the same rut. I knew I had to do something to get myself out of this existential crisis, so I looked for positive input through a combination of helplessness and wild determination.

I came across a book by the German author and life coach Veit Lindau, which provided me with an initial spark. During this time, I also started to work with a "success journal" for the first time. In the beginning, it was a feeble attempt. "Well, it can't hurt," I thought. But I soon began to see that it made a big difference. It wasn't so much the physical journal itself, but rather the consistent focus on mindfulness, my personality, my goals, and the steps I needed to take to achieve them that made a difference. Suddenly, everything came into sharp focus, and it all seemed so simple. I had unlocked the secret!

Today, upon reflection, I now know that I was missing a critical tool to help me give my life a constant direction and to permanently implement positive routines, habits, and rituals in my life. I needed a companion to create the necessary structure, so I created this *Success Journal*, because even though all the other types of journals (seven in total) that I used and tested helped, none of them was the *perfect* fit for me. So, I started to experiment—figuring out what worked and what didn't—to develop this journal over many months.

I have read, listened, searched, collected, tried, discarded, added, eliminated, combined, and included the essence of what I've learned from wise people and from my own life experiences into this *Success Journal*. The process was like white-water rafting. Once I thought I had everything under control—*splash*—a strong wave would hit me in the face. However, I eventually swam into calmer waters, and realized that my *Success Journal* had everything I needed to stay focused and create an upward tract for my life.

I originally developed this journal purely for myself. My main goal was to use it as a rock solid, ritual guide and gave myself these three mini-goals: (1) use it consistently, (2) in the morning, and (3) every day. Today, this journal is an incredibly valuable survival tool in my personal life. If I don't use it, I feel like something is missing in my day and that I'm losing direction. My hope is that you, too, will benefit from this inspirational springboard into positive thinking and personal development.

I don't claim that my *Success Journal* is better or more helpful than other journals of its kind, but rather it simply has its own philosophy. It's designed to be used *once* a day, in the *morning*, for about *ten to fifteen minutes*. I have incorporated my findings from other journals, as well as feedback from some of my fellow *Success Journal* users—to whom I am very grateful. My writing has also been influenced by motivational authors such as Stephen R. Covey, Anthony Robbins, Rolf Dobelli, Earl Nightingale, Gary Keller, and Hal Elrod.

Although Confucius's quote that "the journey is the destination" would have gotten an ignorant yawn from me when I was younger, within this incredibly simple sentence lies an all-encompassing truth: there's nothing more rewarding or powerful than staying on course. There will be days when you will feel great and determined, and there will be days when you feel so-so or not motivated. But, you must always *keep going*!

Working with this *Success Journal* is an extraordinarily effective tool for personality development and for leading a constructive, successful, structured, and fulfilled life. It's so simple, you almost won't believe it!

My hope is that you'll come to think of the *Success Journal* as your faithful companion, a valuable resource to making you as happy and successful as you want to be. Before you begin, keep in mind that the *Success Journal* is a journaling tool and not an agenda, calendar, or organizer, and also please don't forget that the value of this journal is only accessible to *you*, through YOUR constant COMMITMENT.

I encourage you to embark on this journey with optimism, hope, and passion in your heart. Your journey is your destination!

Good luck,
Matthias Hechler

INTRODUCTION

Are you someone who is challenged by the daily grind of life? Do you have many tasks, a lot of responsibilities, and too little time? If you still want to make progress, achieve goals, and enjoy a satisfying life, this journal is your survival tool! Here's how journaling with the *Success Journal* works. You will:

- ✓ Establish a consistent routine (you only need ten to fifteen minutes once a day in the morning—or, if you prefer, in the evening).
- ✓ Program your subconscious mind to focus on your goal through daily written repetitions.
- ✓ Strengthen your "why" so that your motivation constantly has new fuel.
- ✓ Perform daily actions that get you closer to your goal.
- ✓ Always know what to keep your focus on.
- ✓ Work on a vision that acts like a lighthouse for you (see page 32).
- ✓ Develop power questions that will help you in difficult moments.
- ✓ Define and live your core values.
- ✓ Appreciate what makes you grateful, happy, successful, and proud.
- ✓ Do something for yourself and others every day.
- ✓ Expose self-critical beliefs and transform them into positive ones.
- ✓ Break old habits and face new challenges..
- ✓ Continuously question and optimize your thinking, feeling, and behavior.

This journal has one core principle: an easy, constant routine. This is the key to permanently integrating this new habit into your life. That's why it is structured in such a way so that you perform the same ritual once a day, preferably in the morning, which will help you focus on your life visions and goals until you have achieved them.

How about a new morning ritual?

The *Success Journal* is designed to enable you to fill out and write down everything for the day in one sitting. You can also work on it throughout the day or
whichever times work best for you. However, I like to take ten to fifteen minutes
in the morning to write and reflect with it, which is my recommendation to you.
I then take the journal with me to work and review it throughout the day. Every
now and then, when I feel stuck with certain questions, I leave them empty in the
morning, think about them during the day, and then answer them later.

You won't be required to do extra tasks that will only take up more time.

The journaling part of the *Success Journal* is designed for consistency, so there
are no surprises waiting for you. For example, if you have to do something that
you didn't expect or schedule, there is a good chance that you won't do it at all.
This is why there are daily reflection questions and not separate reflection tasks.
Of course, you are free to go the extra mile and invest more time and energy
on your reflections, which is why there is extra space for your writing in the
Thoughts, Ideas & Notes sections.

You can always fill in the entries of your core values and vision beforehand in
preparation for your journaling, or write something down as soon as you think
of it, or even schedule in some extra writing time—but you don't have to. Journal
once a day, every day. That's it. You'll quickly see that motivation is what gets you
started, but an established habit will keep you going.

What you harvest today comes from yesterday's seed of thinking, feeling, and
behavior. What do you want to reap tomorrow?

Throughout this process you will feel supported, not overwhelmed.

Many journals often suggest an evening routine that includes questions such as "What have I learned today?", "What will I do better tomorrow?", or "What special moments have I experienced today?" However, I often found that these types of questions left me feeling inadequate, as if there were something wrong with me if I couldn't answer them, which is why I decided to leave out evening reflections altogether in this journal.

From my personal experience, I find that my days and evenings are much busier than my mornings, and it's not easy for me to make time to write entries every night. Does this sound familiar? You come home late and fall into bed exhausted, or you may have guests over. Maybe you sometimes fall asleep on the couch like I often do. Or maybe you are just drained, and don't want to be bothered with anything in the evening, or perhaps you're busy with a project—like I was when writing this *Success Journal*—and working until late at night.

Even though I tried my best, I just could not find a way to integrate journaling into my evenings. And the fact that I didn't fill in the journal's pages gave me a feeling of failure. I couldn't help but feel like I was throwing a wrench into the entire process. Even though the evening approach wasn't working for me, I knew that in order to see results I had to follow a manageable and consistent routine *every, single, day.*

I knew myself, and knew I was more rested in the morning, wide awake, and ready for the day's challenges. In addition, I also knew that I was able to reflect more clearly on the previous day, so I began to create a morning routine. However, if you don't feel the same way, or if you think more clearly at night, you can easily incorporate journaling into your evening routine.

Do less, but be consistent.

Whether you want to train for a marathon or achieve a career goal, I've found that if you start too fast and cram too much into your schedule, you'll get overwhelmed quickly. When I rediscovered running fifteen years ago, despite the fact that I always hated running during my soccer days as a child and teenager, I had a real "a-ha" moment. Up until this revelation, jogging for me was synonymous with "run as fast as possible." The result: I overexerted myself and stopped running. I needed to learn to be patient.

Since the "faster is better" approach wasn't working, I tried something new during one of my runs. When I came to a long ascent, I *reduced* both my speed and the pressure on my legs to an extent that still allowed me to continue running. Even though it was at a snail's pace, I kept going without feeling depleted of energy. This small change made a huge impact. Even more than the physical effect, I realized that it's sometimes wiser to do less, just enough to get you going and integrate your goal—whatever it may be—firmly into your life. That's the key! The desire for a more intense performance will follow on its own.

Forget discipline; instead, create routines and establish habits.

What do you think of when you hear the word "discipline"? For me, it sounds like effort, willpower, and self-denial. Is that how you feel, too? The word "habit" sounds much nicer, doesn't it? "Routine" and "ritual" do, too. Even though these words have similar meanings, I found that talking about positive routines and habits instead of "discipline" put me in a better frame of mind.

I used to think I wasn't disciplined enough if I couldn't implement positive change permanently, even though other people considered me to be a very consistent and goal-oriented person. With the *Success Journal*, you'll find that it's easier to do what is necessary for your success because it supports you every day and motivates you to *write things down*. This makes a huge difference. Try it out!

The gentle power of a morning routine.

I don't claim to know what an ideal daily routine should look like. However, from my own experience, as I mentioned earlier, I highly recommend that you establish one. It's almost meditative for me when I'm in the flow of my morning routine.

On work days, I start my routine by making my bed and folding my pajamas. I deliberately do both tasks very neatly. After I have taken care of my daughters' lunches for school, I sit down with a glass of water and my favorite smoothie. Then I listen to an audio book or a podcast while taking care of household chores. This routine ends a couple of hours later, after a shower, another glass of water, a cup of coffee, and a maximum of fifteen minutes writing in this journal. After that, my mindset is exactly where I want it to be.

Although my morning routine may seem strange to some, it prepares me for the day and for the tasks that lie ahead of me. It's the little things that set us up for success. Small things give me a good feeling and set the desired course for the rest of my day. Try it for yourself. Find your own routine and see what's good for you in the morning, but try to integrate the *Success Journal* into your morning routine. The way you start your day usually determines how the rest of the day will go.

Keep going!

To be honest and realistic, there will always be days, and short phases in life, in which maintaining a fast pace just isn't possible. Let's face it: we're all humans, not robots. It only becomes dangerous when you get completely out of step or lose your momentum entirely.

Therefore, my advice from my own experience is to set your intentions, pace yourself, do not overextend yourself, and *keep going!* A single day might not make much of a difference, but many days will move mountains. When I am on vacation, I usually take a conscious break from this journal. After a short hiatus, I look forward to starting again and getting back to work with enthusiasm.

TIP: Use this journal once a day, but do it *consistently*. Do less, but keep going! This is what gets results. The drive for more "performance" will come on its own. Remember, if you don't start living the future today, it will never come.

SOW
TODAY

—

REAP
TOMORROW

HOW TO USE THE
SUCCESS JOURNAL

———

The *Success Journal* is not a magic book, but an instrument that accompanies you every day and creates positive momentum for you. Everything you need is already inside of you—you just need to bring it out. This journal will help you structure your thoughts, feelings, and intentions by repeatedly writing them down to live a better, more successful life. You can do it! In these next pages I am going to explain how to fill out the daily journal sections.

◎ I'm Working on This Goal Today

Your goals are extremely important because they are like destination coordinates for your navigation system. Through daily repetition, you will concentrate your energy onto your goals again and again. Write down the goal you want to work on in this section. Theoretically, you can change your goal every day, but I don't recommend this! Even if you have several goals, I advise you to prioritize one goal when journaling and simply keep the others in mind. Change your goals cautiously, or you'll lose your focus! What works for me is that I sometimes switch to a private goal on the weekend or while on vacation and then focus on a business goal on working days.

♦ Purpose & Motivation

Your "why," or the reason you want to reach your goal, is very important for your motivation. You must be sure of why you want to accomplish your goal. If you cannot answer the "why" clearly, something's not right. If this is the case, you should ask yourself if it's really *your* goal or if it is a goal determined by others.

In this section you will find seven different questions about your purpose and motivation, which are repeated weekly. This is to make you look at your goal from different angles to strengthen it. Don't always write down the same answers. Instead, try to find other good reasons. This approach will help you build a rock-solid foundation.

Your commitment to your goal is extremely important. Tell at least three people about your goal so that you feel bound to it and are held accountable. You can also consider devising a personal "penalty" when you get off track or making a public commitment on websites like www.stickk.com, which charge money if you do not act or reach your goal (talk about motivation!). By using these methods, you will be more inclined to get going and will resist the urge to backpedal.

🚀 Power

Make it a rule to perform *three actions* every day that either directly or indirectly help you reach your goal. These actions represent the fuel you really need to obtain your goals! However, be careful and do not overload yourself with too many actions. If you place too much weight on your shoulders all at once, it will only make you collapse under the pressure. These power actions could be small mini-goals. For example, you could start reading a book, listen to a podcast, or make an important contact. The main thing is to *keep going*!

You will probably find that some of your power actions will appear very often—if not always—on your daily entries because they represent the main tasks that are needed to achieve your goal for the day. Does it always have to be three? Not at all. If your goal requires one hundred percent focus on a single action, do that one action, because it doesn't make much sense to add a few more actions just to accomplish three things in a day, which will only result in you feeling overwhelmed. However, from my experience three is a good number. This ensures that you don't approach your goal only from one direction. The main idea is to accomplish several power activities per day that contribute to your main goal.

"

TIP: With each new day, check to see if you completed your tasks from the previous day.

⌗ Focus

Your focus is enormously important to achieving your goals. A successful time-management method called the Eisenhower Matrix, or the Urgent-Important Matrix, which many productivity consultants recommend and use, divides daily to-do tasks into the following four, separate quadrants:

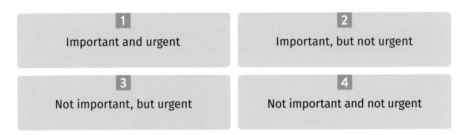

1 Important and urgent	**2** Important, but not urgent
3 Not important, but urgent	**4** Not important and not urgent

If we allow life to just happen, we usually spend most of our time in the first and third quadrants. Unfortunately, the urgent topics are the loudest ones, and the first to greet you in the morning. However, it's the second quadrant that is the most influential to your progress. This means we should accomplish the important tasks today that are not (yet) urgent. However, this requires proactive action and a clear, conscious focus, because second quadrant to-dos don't keep banging on your door. (While speaking about maintaining a successful lifestyle in general, I recommend reading *The Seven Habits of Highly Effective People* by Stephen Covey.)

❶ What is important today?

Think about what is important *today* and write it down in the "What is important today?" framed box. I like to write down what I want to have achieved at the end of the day or which all-decisive task I *have* to get done. Sometimes you might want to include something that builds upon a second goal. Use this framed box in a way that suits you best.

⌗ Focus Questions

Any core values that are simply written down but not achieved serve only as lip service and are worth nothing. This is why you should make a conscious effort to cultivate them. I recommend that you make the daily entries of your core values flexible in terms of time. You don't have to write down a different core value every day in the Focus section. You can also write down the same one for a week or longer, which is actually a good idea because by repeating a core value over several days or weeks you will internalize it more deeply. I often take this approach, but when I feel that a core value is already well integrated into my life, I will write it down only on one day. Remember, the idea is to be *flexible*.

It is possible over a longer period of time that certain core values, such as success, will be your primary focus, and that's perfectly okay. However, you should also keep an eye on other values and not completely neglect them.

☺ How do I feel today?

In the upper right-hand corner there is the question, "How do I feel today?" Take a few moments to observe where you place your checkmark depending on your mood. Perhaps you will notice after some time that you tend to mark the same circles. Does that sound familiar? Maybe you check two circles, or three, tops? Do you say something like this to yourself: "Well, I don't feel bad, but also not great. Maybe only checking five circles is good today."

Why do we do this? The truth is, we usually allow ourselves only a certain level of happiness that is tied with our internal beliefs. The point of this question isn't so much about you logging how you are feeling "for the record," but rather about taking the time to stop and think. Sooner or later, you may realize that you're making a conscious decision to feel happy or unhappy.

Let's suppose your checkmarks are mostly on the second or third circles from the right. This means you're feeling good, but not one hundred percent happy. Maybe at some point you'll start asking yourself what's missing in your life for it to be excellent or for you to feel completely happy. Perhaps you won't be able to find an answer or a reason for it. Then you, like me, will begin to suspect that happiness cannot be a random event that is determined by outside factors, but rather something that you create yourself. You can't *get* happy—you can only *be* happy!

Therefore, I suggest that you be mindful and think about how you answer this question and why each day. I don't deny that there can be circumstances in life that have a considerable influence on the basic conditions for happiness, contentment, and well-being, but nevertheless, you must strive to create your own happiness and consciously decide to be happy every time.

✦ Reflection Questions

Reflection questions are an important instrument to gauge your feelings, thoughts, and actions. Much of what we do happens out of habit and with recurring patterns. We strongly follow our subconscious to decide what we believe about ourselves and other people, in addition to how the world works in general. Later, I will cover more topics that the refection questions will challenge you to think about as well.

If you want to work on your habits, go to Tracking My Habits on page 50.

If we simply allow ourselves to be carried along through life, we almost always follow these unconscious, ingrained patterns of thought and behavior. When you live this way, chances are you will lose orientation and structure in life. The mind wanders, direction becomes vague, and a latent dissatisfaction quickly sets in.

The reflection questions in the *Success Journal* are an important tool not only for your personality development but also for your mental health. Awareness is the first step. It's only when you are aware of something that you can change it.

The five types of reflection questions:

| Kick-Off Reflection | Weekly Reflection | Monthly Reflection | Quarterly Reflection | Final Reflection |

At first, you'll start with a Kick-Off Reflection (pages 52–53). Three and sometimes four repetitions of Weekly Reflection questions are followed by Monthly Reflection questions that are repeated three times (pages 102–115; 166–179; and 246–259). Each of these blocks is seven days long. Finally, the journal then concludes with Quarterly Reflection questions (page 262–275) and Final Reflection questions (pages 276–277). You will notice that the division into week, month, and quarter is not entirely precise, as some questions need to be repeated more often, while others only now and then.

Following each Weekly Reflection question sets are Thoughts, Ideas & Notes pages, which can be used to write down additional reflections, brainstorms, or visualizations if you run out of space.

You will find four reflection questions every day. These are phrased as open questions, so that you cannot simply answer "yes" or "no," but, instead, you will have to really *think* about your answer. There is a constructive follow-up question that gently leads you to an improvement.

⟨⟨ Challenge Questions

Within the weekly reflection questions, you will find some that ask, "What can I do that is new or unfamiliar?" These are your Challenge Questions—new actions or behaviors that will challenge you to break out of your comfort zone. In adulthood, we like to settle in and make ourselves comfortable. We often experience the same thing day in and day out in our weekly rat race. The psychologist Mihály Csíkszentmihályi, who has dedicated himself to flow research, emphasizes how important it is for us to spend time on new, unusual tasks and accept challenges that will make us happy and help us grow.

Collect ideas that will help you extend yourself beyond your usual comfort zone and make a list of them on the Thoughts, Ideas & Notes pages. Remember, don't push yourself too hard; they can be simple, small things like dressing differently, visiting a new place, or watching a documentary about a topic you know nothing about.

◉ Mindfulness

In 2011, I was introduced to a gratitude practice during a coaching session. I had to write down at least five things I was grateful for and five successes every night before going to bed. Five different things every day! After a few weeks of this, I gave up, completely frustrated. I was tired, and I felt like an ungrateful, undisciplined, and unsuccessful failure because I could hardly think of anything— and certainly not something different every day.

Some people say we should be grateful for at least three things every day. However, I don't agree. More isn't always better, and all is not going to be well just because you can quickly rattle off some things you are grateful for every day. If overused, this tactic loses its power. Quality is more important than quantity. Being truly grateful—with awareness and real emotion—for one thing every day is far better than being half-heartedly grateful for three or five different things.

Try it yourself! Write in the space "I am grateful and happy because . . . " regularly. I notice an incredibly warm, pleasant, happy feeling when I am grateful for something.

✛ Inner Strength

In this section, you will find seven different adjectives to complete a series of sentences. This will help you explore your inner strength from different angles, which becomes a lasting self-confirmation. The phrase "I am . . . because" should help you complete the sentence more easily.

Some people find it difficult to feel successful, strong, or proud. If you agree, try it anyway and play around with it. Every human being embodies these inner qualities, but we often don't see or recognize them in ourselves. Immerse yourself as deeply as possible in these feelings and bring them to life.

♛ Mindset

Not every day can be perfect, and circumstances that make life difficult are inevitable. The goal isn't to gloss over everything with a "Yes, I can" mentality, but to start each day with a good, positive attitude. Regardless of whether the sun is shining, or it is raining in your life, you have the power to decide how to start your day.

🎁 Good Deeds

I know how quickly you can forget yourself and others when you put your whole heart into something and get tunnel vision. But you should never neglect self-care, because the only way you can do something for other people is if you're okay. This is why you should do something for yourself every day. It doesn't have to be a big thing. You can treat yourself to an ice cream, take a five-minute stroll outside, place a candle on your desk, or go for a run. Whatever you do, take care of yourself!

In the hustle and bustle of everyday life, don't forget to nurture your relationships and connections to the world. When you do something for other people, you automatically do something for yourself. Positive psychology research shows that we are happier and more fulfilled when we are kind to others.

If you're having trouble coming up with new ways to show others you care, simply focus on what you're already doing. You can show your love by working hard to supplement the household income, making homecooked meals, or driving your kids to their after-school activities. It's also a gift when you hold your loved ones in your arms or simply give someone a heartfelt compliment. It's that easy!

☀ Successes, Pleasures & Opportunities

Every day, give yourself some time and space to write down your successes, pleasant things, or opportunities that present themselves. Make note of anything positive in your day. Although you won't always find great triumphs, it's worthwhile to pay closer attention to the seemingly small things.

This section is meant to be flexible. If you really have to stretch to find three successes or happy moments in a given day, you'll only wind up feeling worse. But if you can easily write down something positive, no matter how small it is, then do it. The key here is to refrain from writing something down just to fill the space.

66

TIP: Keep an eye on the goals or tasks you haven't accomplished. Have you made a note of something you want to do for another person but have yet to put it into practice? Then, write it down again and don't jump to something else. Did you forget to do one of your daily actions? Put it back on your agenda for the following day. Once you've repeated this cycle a few time—even if it's annoying at first—it will force you to get it done. Also try using the reminder function on a smartphone, which serves as a very useful "extra" reinforcement that can help.

It doesn't matter if you keep writing down the same successes, pleasure, and opportunities. Sometimes, I repeat these for weeks. By writing them down several times, I consciously think about them every day and internalize them.

YOUR CORE VALUES, BELIEFS, LIFE VISION & GOALS

Core Values

—

When you define your core values, you build a secure foundation for your daily actions and build a clear path for important decisions. They become the basis for your life and your integrity. You'll gain more clarity about yourself, define your priorities more clearly, and give insight into what you want out of life. You will be able to see what your life is all about when you can define them. This clarity will make it easier for you to cultivate and say "yes" to certain areas of your life and say "no" to others.

I found the inspiration and tools to identify my core values in the bestseller *The Seven Habits of Highly Effective People*. Author Stephen Covey advises readers to develop a model of personal values—a type of "personal constitution" for what is important to you and on which principles you base your life.

Defining your core values doesn't have to be rigid. Maybe in time you will notice aspects that you have overlooked. Or perhaps you will find that a value seems important in your head but is difficult to integrate into everyday life. If this is the case, maybe that core value doesn't belong to you the way you thought it did. Although the priority of your core values can change, you'll find that there will be ones that are fundamentally important in your life. Chances are you're not going to always be one hundred percent true to your core values, but they will continue to serve as guideposts leading you in the right direction.

An emotional approach is very important in this area. What you formulate as your core values should trigger a resounding "yes" deep inside. If this is not the case, then your core values are like pieces of jewelry in a glass cabinet. You can look at them and admire them, but you cannot feel, touch, or wear them.

On the contrary, core values such as "love" are vague and abstract by nature and can be interpreted in different ways. So, I have noticed that this process works better when you convert your values into fundamental principles and rules of conduct. I advise you to not only identify your core values, but also find a fundamental principle that that is associated with it and which is more action-oriented.

Examples of the connection between core values and fundamental principles:

◈ **Core Value:**   Hope
💬 **Fundamental principle:**   I always believe that everything will be all right!

◈ **Core Value:**   Affection
💬 **Fundamental principle:**   I give my love to others.

◈ **Core Value:**   Success
💬 **Fundamental principle:**   My seeds of today are the harvest of tomorrow.

◈ **Core Value:**   Honesty
💬 **Fundamental principle:**   You can count on me to be truthful.

You can have different fundamental principles for the same core value, or you can have principles that represent various facets of your life. It could also be the case that a certain value resonates differently for you in different phases of your life.

TIP: Take time for personal introspection and think about what is important to you. What do you stand for? Write down anything that comes to mind. Is it love, success, hope, freedom, justice, or service? Or is it something completely different? Take your time, and over a few days or week a picture of what's important to you will come into focus.

It is better to define fewer core values and really live them; otherwise, there will be a gap between how you want to live and reality. If you "only" have three to five, then great! In the end, what counts is that you integrate these core values into your life.

My Core Values & Principles
CHARACTER STRENGTHS

1

◆ **Core Value:** CREATIVITY

💬 **Fundamental Principle:** CREATIVITY
TO SEE BEYOND THE BOX

2

◆ **Core Value:** LOVE OF LEARNING

💬 **Fundamental Principle:** NEVER STOP! THERE IS SO
MUCH MORE; FUN, CURIOUS, INTERESTING
STUFF OUT THERE!

3

◆ **Core Value:** PERSEVERANCE

💬 **Fundamental Principle:** YA HAVE TO KEEP WORKING
UNTIL THE REWARD SUDDENLY SHOWS UP!

4

◆ **Core Value:** ZEST FOR LIFE

💬 **Fundamental Principle:** WOW WHAT A RIDE!

5

◆ **Core Value:** KINDNESS

💬 **Fundamental Principle:** DO UNTO OTHERS...

TIP: I sometimes phrase an inspirational
motto as a fundamental principle (e.g. "Today
I sow the success I want to harvest tomorrow").

6

◆ **Core Value:** LEADERSHIP

💬 **Fundamental Principle:** YOU KNOW IT, STRIVE FOR PERFECTION.

7

◆ **Core Value:** SELF - REGULATION

💬 **Fundamental Principle:** CONTROL AND RESTRAINT

8

◆ **Core Value:** GRATITUDE

💬 **Fundamental Principle:** THANKFUL FOR SOOOO MANY GIFTS AND BLESSINGS

9

◆ **Core Value:**

💬 **Fundamental Principle:**

10

◆ **Core Value:**

💬 **Fundamental Principle:**

Beliefs

In this journal, you'll find that the weekly reflection questions ask about negative and self-critical beliefs. Your beliefs can either limit your potential or open the gates to the world. The choice is yours. Our beliefs are generated throughout the course of our lives through education, media, experiences, and defining moments—both positive and negative. The tricky thing is that over time we hardly question or even notice them, because internal beliefs are an intricate part of who we are.

Reveal your negative and self-critical beliefs.

Negative and self-critical beliefs can limit you, restrain you, and ultimately make you unhappy. But positive, affirmative beliefs can have the opposite effect—helping you live a free, self-determined, fulfilling life. Therefore, it's the beliefs that limit you in a destructive way that are the problem.

Some common negative beliefs include:
- 👎 I'm stupid.
- 👎 I can't handle money.
- 👎 I'll never make it.
- 👎 Nobody loves me.
- 👎 Life is unfair.
- 👎 I always get lied to and cheated on.
- 👎 Money spoils my character.
- 👎 Bad weather makes me depressed.
- 👎 I don't sleep well during a full moon.

Many of us automatically reiterate our negative beliefs out loud without even thinking about it, which is why it's important to be more aware of them. When you become conscious of your negative and self-critical beliefs, you have the power to change them.

You may have beliefs that aren't necessarily connected to a concrete phrase. In this case, it's helpful to also pay attention to your default, go-to response of how you react to certain situations or circumstances to see if there is an underlying self-critical belief or pattern behind your behavior.

Write down any self-critical beliefs and replace them with positive ones.

Listen to your thoughts and flag the negative ones in your mind. Once you get used to doing this, you will become better at filtering out self-destructive beliefs. It helps to write them down as soon as you notice them—you will see that this action alone is extremely valuable.

When a self-destructive belief rushes into your head, ask yourself if it's an accurate reflection of your reality. "Is my life really like this?" And if the answer is "yes," then ask yourself "why?" In time, you will be able to consciously correct or stop a negative belief and replace it with a positive thought. Because our beliefs are so deeply rooted inside of us, it will take some time and patience for new and positive thoughts to become an automatic reaction to your life circumstances and situations.

66

TIP: There is a designated place in the *Success Journal* for you to record your beliefs in the middle of the journaling section entitled *Beliefs* (pages 164–165), which is a place where you can identify any negative and self-critical beliefs and replace them with new, positive ones.

When I notice a negative or self-critical belief, I observe it for a certain amount of time, reflecting on how it came to be. Once I have more clarity around its origin, I try to replace it with a positive and constructive belief. For me, I'm careful not to replace it with an unrealistic, flowery, beautifully colored affirmation because my subconscious mind won't take it seriously. Instead, I choose words and phrases that I can truly accept and embrace. It's about what I believe, not what I'm trying to tell myself.

Power Questions

Answering power questions can help boost your mood within seconds. They can pull you in a desired direction and positively influence your mindset. Especially in moments when you tend to lose orientation or get confused, these questions can help you find your way back.

Conscious questions can help you.

How satisfied are you with your relationships with the people you care about? How fulfilling are they for you? I bet you just thought about your answers to these questions. Science tells us that our brains will immediately try to answer a question once it's presented. We can take advantage of our brains' natural tendency by asking ourselves specific questions repeatedly. This is a great tool when doubts, ambiguity, or pessimism wears you down. Having a bad day? Ask the right power question, and you'll be back on your feet in no time. Are you bombarded by negative emotions? Your power questions will give you the energy you need to surmount them. Do you feel like you don't know anything anymore? With your power questions, you will find the answers you need.

To give you an example, here are some of my power questions:

- ❓ What would the person I want to be do now?
- ❓ How do I have to act now to be satisfied on my deathbed?
- ❓ What is the next important step right now?
- ❓ What would I recommend to my best friend in this situation?
- ❓ What can I do now to get one step closer to my goal?
- ❓ What is the good thing about the situation I am experiencing right now?

Your power questions can—and most likely will—change over time. When you work with them, you will get a better feel for which types of questions are the most helpful. I've found that it helps to include a positive meaning or a personal benefit in my questions.

Do you know those moments that change everything and leave a groundbreaking impact on you? I was in this type of situation when I heard author and life coach Veit Lindau ask the following questions: "How does the person who has already achieved a goal think, feel, and act?" and "How would the person I want to be act now?" These questions had an incredible and direct effect on me. Since hearing them, I have tried to work with them consciously as often as possible.

> **TIP:** You can experiment with your power questions, especially in situations where you are trying to consciously construct questions and test their effect on you. You will sense if they're lifting you up or bringing you down. If you have some power questions that come to mind already, write them down below and internalize them. Remember, less is more. It only takes three to five questions to help yourself in most situations.

My Power Questions:

- WHAT CAN I DO RIGHT NOW TO GET ONE STEP CLOSER TO MY GOAL

Life Vision: Building Your Own Lighthouse

To avoid setting empty goals that aren't fulfilling, you need to know your core values and have a vision for your life. Your goals should lead you along a path to a larger, more comprehensive idea of your life. Your life vision is your lighthouse, helping you determine the position of your goals again and again. Your life vision should carry you for at least the next five years.

What kind of person do you want to be?

What do you want to wake up for in the morning? How do you want to live? Who will you be in five years? What will you be doing in five years? What will you have in five years? If you can already see a clear vision of your life, great! But if you don't know where to go or how to get there, it's okay. Just like discovering your core values and beliefs, a life vision is something that often needs some time and consideration. Although you can start working on a goal without a life vision, it's important in the long run that your inner fire is fueling your goals.

Start now and you can work out the details as you go. Your life vision can mature over time, which will result in new goals. Soon enough, your vision of life will be manifested in the here and now. Make sure to include a time frame in which you want your life vision to come to fruition (a specific month and year). I like to write in the present tense, as if my life vision is already a reality.

Make your life vision visible.

You can also create visual elements or a mood board for your life vision! Pictures that inspire and motivate you are very effective, for obtaining both your life vision and your goals. Look for images that include specific elements of your vision; there is no limit to your imagination. The important thing is to choose images that inspire you when you look at them.

If the space in this journal is not enough to hold your visual elements, you can make a life vision mood board or choose another method that suits you. I like to create a mind map in which I placed pictures, photos of role models, and some graphics and phrases that represent my vision around a photo of me in the center.

Are you moving "away" from or "toward" something?

In my opinion, there is no rule about how to set up your life vision. Rolf Dobelli, author of *The Art of Acting Smart*, talks about "via negativa," which originally comes from the theology concept that one cannot say what God *is*, only what he/she is *not*. This concept is like Michelangelo's claim to have chipped away everything that was not *David* when he created his famous statue.

So, if it's difficult for you to define a concrete vision for your life, then concentrate on what you *don't* want. What can you get rid of in your life? It's usually quite easy to list what no longer serves us. So, write it all down. Then rephrase it in a positive way. I have heard from very successful people on several occasions that they use this same exact process to achieve their life vision. Give it a try!

"

TIP: Remember, you don't need a "perfect" life vision. Just begin, even if it's a little at first. You will see more clearly what it is you desire as time goes on. For a long time, I only had vague visions of my future life. Actually, they were more like dreams, because I didn't do anything to get closer to them—they were always off in the future. Don't make the mistake I did and think that it will happen by itself someday. Write down your life vision, make it visible, and live it.

In the quarterly reflection pages, you will find a question about what separates you from your life vision. It helps to ask yourself how the person you see in your life vision thinks, acts, feels, and behaves. Bring this persona into your life as much as you can.

My Life Vision

How am I?

GETTING BETTER EVERY DAY!
I MEAN IT! 😃

How do I feel?

What do I experience?

> If a man takes no thought about what is distant, he will find sorrow near at hand.
>
> — Confucius

How do I act?

_____
_____
_____
_____
_____
_____
_____

Whom do I surround myself with?

_____
_____
_____
_____
_____
_____
_____

What do I own?

_____
_____
_____
_____
_____
_____
_____

My Wheel of Life Diagram

Define eight areas
of your life and write
them each in a box.

Now, give each area a rating
from 1 (very bad) to 10
(perfect). When you connect
the dots with a line, notice
how even or out-of-center
your life is at the moment.
This diagram will let you see
where you may need more
work or concentration and
also gives an additional
point of reference for
identifying your goals.

TIP: Create your wheel of life
diagram (1) at the beginning
of your goal journey and (2)
then again at the end. Use
two different colors for each
period to see the difference.

Example:

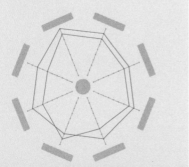

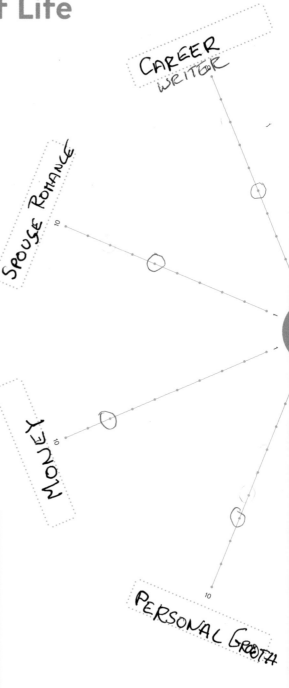

CAREER
WRITER

SPOUSE ROMANCE

10

MONEY
10

PERSONAL GROOTH
10

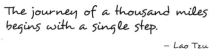

HEALTH
10

PHYSICAL ENVIRONMENT
10

FUN & RECREATION
10

FAMILY & FRIENDS
10

**Examples for your
areas of life:**

Family
Finance
Fitness
Fun and Leisure
Friendship
Health
Network
Partnership
Personal Development
Professional Development
Well-being
Work and Business

My Wish List

Wishes, dreams, and goals are closely linked. Write down everything you want to achieve, experience, or desire. Let loud and quiet thoughts bubble to the surface—this is your time to collect ideas. You can also list rewards for achieved goals. On the following pages, you will choose five goals you want to work on.

Think about your vision, which you will define in this journal. Your individual goals should lead you there!

GET A HOUSE AT RAINTREE

Body and Health

KEEP GETTING HEALTHIER AND SEE WHERE I CAN GO WITH CLOTHES SIZES.

Home

WE'VE DONE A LOT THIS YEAR WISH WOULD BE A SPRINTER MAYBE ADD A LOG CABIN SOMEDAY

Professional Development

BE RECOGNIZED AS AN AUTHOR THAT PEOPLE WANT TO READ

Work and Business

FINISH WRITING MY FIRST
BOOK

Material Possessions and Finances

EARN ENOUGH WITH THE
FIRST BOOK TO EASILY
PAY FOR A NEW DEISEL
TRUCK AND NEW SPRINTER

Experiences

- ROUTE 66
- BRING ALL THE KIDS OCEANSIDE

Partnership, Family, and Friends

MORE ROMANCE
MORE GATHERINGS

Goal Setting

Motivational author Jack Canfield said, "People who don't have goals work for people who do." And there is certainly some truth to this quote since today's leaders, teachers, and life coaches agree that individuals must work toward a goal in order to be happy.

The importance of goal setting.

In his book *What They Don't Teach You at Harvard Business School*, author Mark H. McCormack talks about a 1979 study of students in the Harvard MBA program that showed how much of an impact goal setting has on our quality of life. Students were asked if they had set goals for their future and made any plans on how to achieve them. The results were:

- 3 percent of the students had written down defined goals and plans
- 13 percent had goals, but did not write them down
- 84 percent had no defined goals

Ten years later the MBA students were questioned again. Here's what researchers found:

- On average, the 13 percent with goals earned twice as much as the ones without goals.
- But remarkably, the 3 percent who had written their goals down earned *ten times* more than the remaining 97 percent of participants combined!

Another study by Dr. Gail Matthews of the Dominican University of California also showed that people who define and write down their goals are more successful than people who do not.

The journey is the real destination.

Many people associate goals with blind ambition or focus on material things that aren't representative of their core values. But goals are anything that pertains to an individual. You may want to redesign your living room, become self-employed, expand a company, lose weight, run a half-marathon, or earn six figures. Whatever it may be, goals are as unique as the people who chase them.

Life coach Veit Lindau writes in his book *Werde verrückt (Go Crazy)* that at some point in a person's life they reach the realization that it is not a question of achieving a goal, but rather of who they need to become in order to achieve it. Everyone who has set out on this path and achieved his or her goals understands what Lindau means.

It took me a long time to realize that the *achievement* of my goals wouldn't make me happy or successful. Once you arrive at your destination, you will rejoice and celebrate your accomplishment—but this joy is short-lived. How long will this feeling of euphoria last? A day? A week? A month? Soon enough, your achievement becomes the norm—and those who define themselves exclusively by their goals are left feeling empty.

It's a conscious, mindful path toward goals that leads us to a greater vision of our lives and that brings us lasting fulfillment. We need these goals to be on our path. Otherwise, we'd simply be drifting without a plan.

It's an illusion that success lies in the future.

I held on to a belief early on—in the distant future—that one day I would achieve a big breakthrough or huge success, and only then would I be happy. This is a farce. Although I held on to the idea that I needed to reach "an end point," I came to realize that this is ridiculous because life goes on even after you reach your goal.

I now realize that my goal is not somewhere out there in the future, because the "future" is going to be the *present* at some point. And when I do reach my goal, it won't define me as a "successful person." Rather, I will have reach my goal because I already *am* this person.

If you don't want to run the risk of pushing your goals into the future, you have to start thinking, feeling, and acting as *if* you've already achieved them.

Values, visions, and missions serve as goal amplifiers.

It is important that your goal is consistent with your vision and core values. Only then can you pursue it with the inner fire you need to find fulfillment in the goal itself, and on the path that leads you there. A goal that is in harmony with your personal values and vision is like a looking glass through which your life comes into focus. These components are the basics, which is why they are included throughout this journal.

It also helps if you can define a "mission" that acts as a link between your goals and your vision. If you want to do this, first ask yourself which emotional heading would best describe the path you want to take. Whether this is a short- or long-term view doesn't matter. What's important is that it gives you a direction.

Which period should you choose for your goals?

I recommend that you tackle goals that can be achieved in a period from two weeks at a minimum and to one year at the maximum. The structure of the *Success Journal* fits best into this time frame. If you are pursuing a longer-term goal, divide it into parts that you can accomplish in less time.

You should always have a clear view of what you can do for your goal *today*. If you cannot, the goal may be too far away and therefore still too vague in the present. It's best to give yourself two to three months to achieve your goal.

Your goal may come from an unexpected place.

The resolution of your goal does not always come from where you initially expected. If you have "programmed" your goal coordinates, it's still possible that you may have to take a few detours to reach your destination.

Trust in your subconscious mind to attract what you need to get to your goal. Focus on the "what" but be open to the "how." I have experienced, more than once, times in which I came across something seemingly unimportant but was transported—like a pinball—to another destination, and this chain of events brought me decisively further toward my goal. When I look back, I realize that without this inconspicuous impulse I would never have reached where I am now. You never know where things come from or what's in it for you. Therefore, be open and trust your intuition.

The SMART Formula for Your Goals

Your goals should be SMART, meaning that they are phrased in a way that helps you achieve them.

Write your goals so that they are *Specific* (accurately described), *Measurable* (able to be measured with exact metrics), *Attractive* (desirable), *Realistic* (challenging but achievable), and *Timed* (an exact date of achievement). It is especially important that there is a date attached to your goal so that it is measurable. It is best to write down your goal in the present tense, because this is how your subconscious mind understands it best.

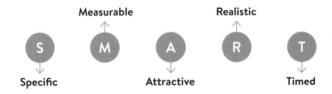

So, don't say:	"I'm going to save a lot of money."	
Instead try something like:	"On December 31, 2021, I will have $20,000 in my savings account."	

> **TIP:** I always integrate a picture, or motif, that appeals to me emotionally into my goal formulation. I like to set a goal collage as my screen saver or print several copies and place them in various locations around my house where I will see them several times a day. Now, that's a lot of extra motivation! Remember to enter your target "goal completion" date in your calendar to hold yourself accountable.
>
> I hope that the *Success Journal* serves you well—giving you clear direction and motivation to achieve your dreams. Remember, anything is possible with the right goals, vision, and a positive mindset in place. You've got this!

My Goals

You can find a goal evaluation on page 278.

You can collect your goals here (remember the SMART formula). Think about how you're going to reward yourself when you reach a goal. But also consider a consequence in case you don't reach it. Don't change your goals too often when journaling, because you could easily get overwhelmed (please also see page 16).

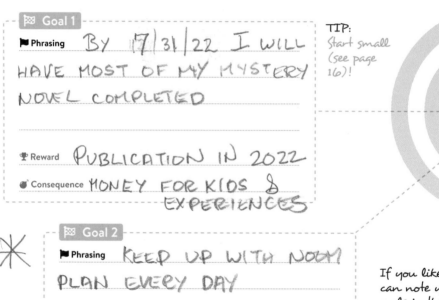

⚑ Goal 1

⚑ Phrasing BY 7/31/22 I WILL HAVE MOST OF MY MYSTERY NOVEL COMPLETED

TIP:
Start small
(see page
16)!

🏆 Reward PUBLICATION IN 2022

⊙ Consequence MONEY FOR KIDS & EXPERIENCES

⚑ Goal 2

⚑ Phrasing KEEP UP WITH NOOM PLAN EVERY DAY
SIZE 16 - THEN SIZE 14

🏆 Reward SILK BLOUSE + CAMEL SLACKS

⊙ Consequence HEALTHIER & MORE ENERGY

If you like, you can note your goals in this timeline and make a plan for the next year.

🚀
Today

Date

| 1 month | 2 months | 3 months | 4 months | 5 months | 6 months |

MY TIMELINE

Goal 3

SHORT TERM

Phrasing TRY ON ALL CLOTHES CULL WARDROBE, MAKE WAY FOR SMALLER SIZES (UNDER BED)

Reward LOOK BETTER IN PUBLIC

Consequence RESPECT

Remember to visualize (see pages 48-49)!

Goal 4

Phrasing GET A SMALL HOUSE AT RAINTREE

Reward COMFORTABLE PLACE

Consequence

Goal 5

Phrasing

Reward

Consequence

Visualization

Virtually all trainers regard the visualization of goals as an extremely important component for their achievement. Athletes, speakers, managers, actors—everyone who has to deliver top performance works with the visualization process. In principle, we all visualize more or less constantly. That's what you might call a "mental movie." As a rule, however, we surrender ourselves to what "mental movies" just happen to be shown in our heads. Only rarely do we proactively shape this in the direction we want over a longer period of time repeatedly and in a focused manner.

How should you visualize?

Visualization is about imagining your achieved goal or the successful process intensively and emotionally in your mind. It's the only language our subconscious understands. Through our thinking and behavior, our subconscious attracts the circumstances that get us to our goals.

If you want, you can work with multiple visualizations for your goal. However, I usually only use one and direct all my energy into it. It is important that you feel joy and distinct emotions when visualizing. You have to enjoy doing it. If you only do it reluctantly, you probably won't do it repeatedly over a longer time. Again, keep going until you find the solution that suits you.

Don't make the mistake I did of seeing visualization as too dogmatic. I used to think I had to imagine exactly what my "finish line" would look like—and as joyfully as possible. What resulted was forced pictures with artificial inner joy. There's no use in that! Your visualization is good when your pulse rises and you feel an inner excitement.

You can also try to enhance the colors in your mind or touch objects to intensify the visualization.

How often should you visualize?

It is often recommended to visualize two or three times a day for a few minutes—preferably in alpha state (i.e., when you are very relaxed), such as in the morning and in the evening in bed. If that works for you—great!

Mostly, I visualize only once a day, but for 5 to 10 minutes. For me, visualization is a fixed ritual during my morning shower, which I always look forward to. It took me a while to find this format for myself. Find out what works best for you, too.

Music is the fuel for your visualization.

What can help a lot with visualization is the support of music. While directing my own success movie in my mind, I visualize the whole story from the present to the achievement of my goals. Then fragments of pictures race past my mind and strong emotions arise. Just try it, and maybe it'll help you too. Just experiment and search for a suitable song or an entire playlist. For me, this is like searching for a radio station. At first there is only static, white noise, and crackling sounds, the signal is weak, and then suddenly—bam—it is crystal clear and intense.

You'll know instinctively when it fits. On this basis your visualization has real power!

TIP: Build a "visual key point" into your visualization that has a relation to today. It is about having a concrete, visual, and fixed point that slowly transforms from now until the day the goal is reached.

For example, some time ago I had set myself a financial goal for my company. On the whiteboard in my office, I wrote down the current number and updated it again, and again, and again. The number increased each way while I worked toward my target goal. It represented exactly what I integrated into my visualization from the very beginning. I imagined the process of correcting the number over and over until finally my target number remained. This type of positive thinking acts like a bridge connecting the present today to your goal of tomorrow; it gives extra energy to your visualization.

My Visualization

Describe emotionally, in clear pictures and in the present tense the exact moment when you have reached your goal.

What do you see? How do you feel? What's going on? Is someone congratulating you? Are you rewarding yourself for your achievement? Are you holding something in your hands that shows you made it? Or do you celebrate your success with others? Turn your emotional radio to maximum volume!

Try to give the visualization a firm place in your day.

Goal 1:

WHEN SOMEONE HANDS ME MY FIRST
HARD-BACKED EDITION OF MY FIRST
NOVEL.

Goal 2:

WHEN I CAN WEAR A SIZE 12-14
DRESS

> *The mind is everything. What you think you become.*
>
> — Buddha

Goal 3:

WHEN I CROSS THE FINISH LINE
OF THE NEXT 5K (2/26/22

Goal 4:

Goal 5:

TRACKING MY HABITS

Simply enter a habit, write the calendar week above the column, and check the box on the respective day (one column is from Sunday to Saturday).

Habit	WRITING
3/7	

Sun, Mon, Tue, Wed, Thu, Fri, Sat

26 Weeks

Habit	EXERCISE
3/7	

Sun, Mon, Tue, Wed, Thu, Fri, Sat

Habit	JOURNALING
3/7	

Sun, Mon, Tue, Wed, Thu, Fri, Sat

Habit	

Sun, Mon, Tue, Wed, Thu, Fri, Sat

THE
SUCCESS JOURNAL

---

100 DAYS TO A FULFILLED LIFE

FAR FROM
ENOUGH

📅 **Day** » 3/7/2021

Let's go!

I'm working on this goal today ◎ SETTING UP AND WRITING DOWN GOALS

🔥 **Purpose & Motivation**

You should make this a rule with every new goal to hold yourself accountable!

Which three people will I tell about my goal?

🚀 **Power**

What will I do today in order to get closer to my goal?

☑ ORDER A. CHRISTY NOVEL

☑ WRITE A FEW NOTES

☐

⛶ **Focus**

Which of my core values do I want to focus on today?

What is important today?

OUR CHURCH WEDDING ANNIVERSARY ❶❻ YRS

🔆 **Kick-Off Reflection**

To what extent am I clear about the next goals and my vision?

PRETTY DARN CLEAR— WRITING AND NOOM

When do I take the time to think about and define them?

👁 Mindfulness

I am **grateful and happy** because ...

I HAVE:
A GOOD MAN

A WARM, DRY, ATTRACTIVE HOME

NO SHORTAGE OF FOOD

♕ Mindset

Today is going to be **really good** because ...

I TALKED TO FRIENDS AND TO MY FAMILY

IT MAKES ME SMILE AND FEEL GOOD

🎁 Good Deeds

What can I do for myself today?

STAY ON PLAN

EXCERSISE AND WALK

⚙ Successes, Pleasures & Opportunities

PLEASURE: MY NEW JOURNAL

SUCCESS: A GOOD NOOM DAY

OPPORTUNITY: A CHANCE TO GET VACCINE TODAY!
(DONT EVEN FEEL SICK FROM IT)

.... Schedule time for this and ....
note the result on the
respective pages.

⊕ Inner Strength

I am **optimistic** because ...

THERE IS SUNSHINE!

Before you start,
be sure to read
pages 16-21!

What can I do for others today?

SET UP DATE W/KUNY

🖉 Kick-Off Reflection

Which core values and fundamental principles
do I have and how well do I know them?

TENACITY - FOR SOMETHING
I REALLY WANT

When will I take the time to reflect about
and define them?

I'm working on this goal today

(EXERCISE)

WRITING

Repeat your goal here daily and don't change it too often!

🔥 **Purpose & Motivation**

Why do I want to reach this goal?

🚀 **Power**

✅ **Check** Did I complete yesterday's tasks? — YEP

What will I do today in order to get closer to my goal?

☐ WRITE NOTES ON HOW
☐ THE MYSTERY WILL FLOW
☐

⚙ **Focus**

Which of my core values do I want to focus on today?

PERSERVERANCE

What is important today?

⏱ **Weekly Reflection**

What robbed me of energy or did me no good?

BAD SLEEPING SCHEDULE

How can I improve this?

• GET UP AND ACTIVE AT
• SET ALARM   7:30

👁 Mindfulness

I am **grateful and happy** because ...

➕ Inner Strength

I am **successful** because ...

I HAVE STARTED TO FOCUS

👑 Mindset

Today is going to be **wonderful** because ...

I MAY GET TO SPEND TIME W/HUNTER

🎁 Good Deeds

What can I do for myself today?

WRITE NOTES IN THE SUN

What can I do for others today?

☀ Successes, Pleasures & Opportunities

Note these on
pages 164-165.

ⓘ Weekly Reflection

What self-critical beliefs did I notice?

What positive beliefs will I replace them with?

I'm working on this goal today

(EXERCISE

WRITING

🔥 Purpose & Motivation

Who or what can support me on the way to my goal?

NOOM - EATING AT NIGHT

🚀 Power

What will I do today in order to get closer to my goal?

NOT ALL

☑ **Check**
Did I complete yesterday's tasks?

☐ WORK ON NOTES
☐   AND OUTLINE
☐

⦂⦂ Focus

Which of my core values do I want to focus on today?

MORE TENACITY
(FOCUS)

This doesn't have to be a base jump from the Empire State Building! Little things are enough!

What is important today?

TO GET AT LEAST 2 HRS OF WRITING WORK IN

🎯 Weekly Reflection

❝❝ Challenge: What did I do that was new or unfamiliar?

GET THE LLC DISOLVED

❝❝ Challenge: What new or unusual actions am I going to take in the next 7 days?

TRY MY POI BALLS

☹ ⚪ ⚪ ⚪ ⚪ ⚪ ⚪ 😊

👁 Mindfulness

I am **grateful and happy** because ...

I GOT THE LLC OFF
MY BACK

➕ Inner Strength

I am **competent** because ...

👑 Mindset

Today is going to be **excellent** because ...

IT FEELS LIKE A NEW, CLEAN START

🎁 Good Deeds

What can I do for myself today?

PEDICURE

What can I do for others today?

ASK RE: FRIENDS

☀ Successes, Pleasures & Opportunities

THE DARN LLC

⚡ Weekly Reflection

How well did I take care of myself?

MADE PEDI APPNT.

Do I need to make any improvements?

LOOK INTO FUN

I'm working on this goal today

🔥 Purpose & Motivation

What is going to be better when I have reached my goal?

🚀 Power

What will I do today in order to get closer to my goal?

☐
☐
☐

✅ Check
Did I complete yesterday's tasks?

⟦ ⟧ Focus

Which of my core values do I want to focus on today?

What is important today?

🧭 Weekly Reflection

What was particularly good or gave me pleasure?

PAINTED BATHROOM

ORGANIZED PANTRY

How can I cultivate this even more in my life?

STAY FOCUSED

👁 Mindfulness

I am **grateful and happy** because ...

I HAVE FRIENDS, FAMILY
TO SPEND TIME WITH,
AND GRANDKIDS

👑 Mindset

Today is going to be **very special** because ...

THE PLACE IS CLEAN, TIDY, ORGANIZED
ALL VERY PLEASANT! 🙂

➕ Inner Strength

I am **strong** because ...

*How would you feel if
you didn't have this?*
LONELY

🎁 Good Deeds

What can I do for myself today?

What can I do for others today?

☀ Successes, Pleasures & Opportunities

LUNCH
THURSAW KUNY THIS PAST THUR, SHORT VISIT
SUN PAINTED BATHRM A PRETTY SOFT GREEN
FINALLY ONE ROOM THAT ISNT BROWN

➍ Weekly Reflection

When have I felt like a victim or blamed others?

How am I going to handle this better?

I'm working on this goal today

WE HAVE BEEN HOSTING AT STATE PARKS

🔥 Purpose & Motivation

How will I feel when I have reached my goal?

🚀 Power

What will I do today in order to get closer to my goal?

☐
☐
☐

✅ **Check**
Did I complete yesterday's tasks?

⛶ Focus

Which of my core values do I want to focus on today?

See tip on page 27.

What is important today?

🧭 Weekly Reflection

How consistently have I been working on habit(s) lately?

Which habit(s) do I want to work on in the next 7 days?

👁 Mindfulness

I am **grateful and happy** because …

....

....

....

➕ Inner Strength

I am **proud** because …

....

....

....

♛ Mindset

Today is going to be **superb** because …

....

....

🎁 Good Deeds

What can I do for myself today?

....

....

What can I do for others today?

....

....

☼ Successes, Pleasures & Opportunities

....

....

....

You don't have to compulsively work on habits. But you can. ;-)

🧭 Weekly Reflection

How satisfied am I with myself?

....

....

....

What can I do in the next 7 days to be fully satisfied with myself?

....

....

....

I'm working on this goal today.

I HAVE BEEN STAGNENT WITH MY NOOM PLAN. TODAY I AM RAMPING BACK UP

🔥 **Purpose & Motivation**

Who else will benefit when I reach my goal?

HOPEFULLY MY FAMILY

🚀 **Power**

What will I do today in order to get closer to my goal?

- [ ] LOG MEALS / STAY ON GOAL
- [ ]
- [ ]

✓ Check Did I complete yesterday's tasks?

⟦⟧ **Focus**

Which of my core values do I want to focus on today?

A LITTLE SELF-DICIPLINE ABOUT FOOD

What is important today?

TO GET BACK ON TRACK

Have you written down any power questions yet (see page 31)?

⚡ **Weekly Reflection**

What negative thoughts or feelings (fear, envy, anger, etc.) accompanied me?

LACK OF WEIGHT LOSS
UPSET W/ RAE

How can I accept them without letting them take over?

USE OH WELL STATEMENT AND MOVE FORWARD

FIND OUT WHAT'S GOING ON

82421 8

👁 Mindfulness

I am **grateful and happy** because ...

I HAVE AN ADVENTUROUS
LIFESTYLE, AND A
HEALTY HAPPY FAMILY

➕ Inner Strength

I am **determined** because ...

I CAN DO IT

👑 Mindset

Today is going to be **meaningful** because ...

I AM STARTING ANEW!

🎁 Good Deeds

What can I do for myself today?

STICK TO PLAN ONE-DAY-
AT-A-TIME STYLE

What can I do for others today?

FIND OUT WHAT
RACHEL MEANS

☀ Successes, Pleasures & Opportunities

SUCCESS TO GET THIS FAR ...
OPPORTUNITY TO BREAK A BARRIER ...

⚡ Weekly Reflection

How much time have I spent on unnecessary distractions?

ACHIEVEMENT
ADVENTURE
FAMILY

How can I avoid these distractions?

OPTIMISM
ORDER
RESPECT

I'm working on this goal today

5K   2/26/22

Remember your visualization
(see pages 48-49).

🔥 **Purpose & Motivation**

How will I reward
myself when
I have reached
my goal?

BY FINISHING THE RUN!

🚀 **Power**

What will I do
today in order
to get closer
to my goal?

✅ **Check**
Did I complete
yesterday's tasks?

☐ WATCH NOOM PLAN
☐ TRAINING RUN
☐ FOOD PLANING

⟦⟧ **Focus**

Which of my core values do I want
to focus on today?

Wr

What is important today?

DEFINING MY
HAPPINESS

🔘 **Weekly Reflection**

What stressed or annoyed me?

EMOTIONAL TALKS

How can I avoid or improve this?

KEEP TALKING

👁 Mindfulness

I am **grateful and happy** because ...

1 AM HEALTHY
2 I AM STILL ABLE
   TO TRAIN

➕ Inner Strength

I am **persevering** because ...

I WANT TO REACH
THE GOAL OF DOING
A GOOD 5K

👑 Mindset

Today is going to be **brilliant** because ...

I AM GOING TO RUN, KEEP ON PLAN,
PLAN EVENING CALORIES,
      WORK ON BYLAW PROJ.

🎁 Good Deeds

What can I do for myself today?

SEE ABOVE

What can I do for others today?

TEXT KUNY

☀ Successes, Pleasures & Opportunities

🕐 Weekly Reflection

How often have I actually done the tasks
I have planned?

NOT BAD

How can I improve?

WITH LOTS

I'm working on this goal today

1. AT LEAST ONE CHAPTER
2. STRIVE FOR 10000 STEPS

🔥 **Purpose & Motivation**

Think long term and be really pessimistic!

What are the consequences if I don't reach my goal?

1. PERSONAL RECESSION

2. NOT HAVE THE ACTIVE LIFE I WANT.

🚀 **Power**

What will I do today in order to get closer to my goal?

☑ **Check**
Did I complete yesterday's tasks?

☐ WRITE 3-4 HOURS
☐ BUNDLE UP AND WALK
☐

⬚ **Focus**

Which of my core values do I want to focus on today?

What is important today?

TO BUILD ON THE HAPPINESS AND CONTENTMENT I AM FEELING

⏺ **Weekly Reflection**

What have I done for my own development?

What can I do for my development in the next 7 days?

👁 Mindfulness

I am **grateful and happy** because ...

➕ Inner Strength

I am **optimistic** because ...

I AM FINALLY WRITING AGAIN.

👑 Mindset

Today is going to be **really good** because ...

I CHOOSE JOY...

🎁 Good Deeds

What can I do for myself today? QUOTE:

What can I do for others today? I INVITE BILLY TO DINNER.

THE ONLY PERSON YOU SHOULD COMPARE YOURSELF TO IS THE PERSON YOU

☀ Successes, Pleasures & Opportunities

WERE YESTERDAY

🧭 Weekly Reflection

In which situations have I behaved unfavorably?

What should I do instead?

A CLEAR

↓

F[]CUS

↓

LEADS TO TARGETED ACTIONS!

TIP: You can also create a list of ideas for your weekly challenges.

> When it is obvious that the goals cannot be reached, don't adjust the goals, adjust the action steps.
>
> — Confucius

I'm working on this goal today

MAY 1 A GREAT DAY FOR A NEW START

🔥 Purpose & Motivation

Why do I want to reach this goal?

1. FINISH THE BOOK
2. REACH UNDER 200
3. RUN A 5K

Try to find new answers to these questions as often as possible!

✅ **Check** Did I complete yesterday's tasks?

🏹 Power

What will I do today in order to get closer to my goal?

☐ WRITE 2 HOURS TONITE
☐ STAY ON PLAN TODAY
☐ DO THE C·25K

Focus

Which of my core values do I want to focus on today?

TENACITY
SELF VALUE
(DICIPLINE)

What is important today?   JOY!

⏱ Weekly Reflection

What robbed me of energy or did me no good?

COMPUTER GAMES

How can I improve this?

DONT PLAY FOR NOW

👁 Mindfulness

I am **grateful and happy** because …

....

....

....

➕ Inner Strength

I am **successful** because …

....

....

....

👑 Mindset

Today is going to be **wonderful** because …

....

....

....

🎁 Good Deeds

What can I do for myself today?

....

....

What can I do for others today?

....

....

☀ Successes, Pleasures & Opportunities

....

....

....

🧭 Weekly Reflection

What self-critical beliefs did I notice?

....

....

....

What positive beliefs will I replace them with?

....

....

....

I'm working on this goal today

You can change your goals—but with caution; otherwise, you'll get overwhelmed!

🔥 **Purpose & Motivation**

Who or what can support me on the way to my goal?

🚀 **Power**

What will I do today in order to get closer to my goal?

☐
☐
☐

✅ **Check**
Did I complete yesterday's tasks?

⟦⟧ **Focus**

Which of my core values do I want to focus on today?

What is important today?

Collect challenging ideas in a list.

🔄 **Weekly Reflection**

❝❝ Challenge: Did I actually do the tasks I planned and how did it feel?

❝❝ Challenge: What new or unusual actions am I going to take in the next 7 days?

How do I feel today?   ● ● ● ● ● ● ●

👁 Mindfulness

I am **grateful and happy** because ...

....

....

....

➕ Inner Strength

I am **competent** because ...

....

....

....

👑 Mindset

Today is going to be **excellent** because ...

....

....

....

🎁 Good Deeds

What can I do for myself today?

....

....

What can I do for others today?

....

....

☀ Successes, Pleasures & Opportunities

....

....

....

🧭 Weekly Reflection

How well did I take care of myself?

....

....

....

Do I need to make any improvements?

....

....

....

11

18

I'm working on this goal today

🔥 **Purpose & Motivation**

What is going to be better when I have reached my goal?

✈ **Power**

What will I do today in order to get closer to my goal?

✅ **Check**
Did I complete yesterday's tasks?

⟦⟧ **Focus**

Which of my core values do I want to focus on today?

What is important today?

🧭 **Weekly Reflection**

What was particularly good or gave me pleasure?

How can I cultivate this even more in my life?

How do I feel today?   ● ● ● ● ● ● ●

👁 Mindfulness

I am **grateful and happy** because ...

....

....

....

➕ Inner Strength

I am **strong** because ...

....

....

....

👑 Mindset

Today is going to be **very special** because ...   *What would the person you want to be write here?*

....

....

🎁 Good Deeds

What can I do for myself today?

....

....

What can I do for others today?

....

....

☀ Successes, Pleasures & Opportunities

....

....

....

🕐 Weekly Reflection

When have I felt like a victim or blamed others?

....

....

....

How am I going to handle this better?

....

....

....

19

I'm working on this goal today

🔥 Purpose & Motivation

How will I feel when I have reached my goal?

🚀 Power

What will I do today in order to get closer to my goal?

☐
☐
☐

✅ **Check**
Did I complete yesterday's tasks?

[ ] Focus

Which of my core values do I want to focus on today?

What is important today?

🧭 Weekly Reflection

How consistently have I worked on habit(s) in the last 7 days?

Which habit(s) do I want to work on in the next 7 days?

How do I feel today? ● ● ● ● ● ● ●

👁 Mindfulness

I am **grateful and happy** because ...

....

....

....

➕ Inner Strength

I am **proud** because ...

....

....

....

♛ Mindset

Today is going to be **superb** because ...

....

....

🎁 Good Deeds

Also be aware of what you're already doing. ....

What can I do for myself today?

....

....

What can I do for others today?

....

....

☀ Successes, Pleasures & Opportunities

....

....

....

.... You can track this on page 50 if you like.

🧭 Weekly Reflection

How satisfied am I with myself?

....

....

....

What can I do in the next 7 days to be fully satisfied with myself?

....

....

....

I'm working on this goal today

🔥 **Purpose & Motivation**

Who else will benefit when I reach my goal?

🚀 **Power**

What will I do today in order to get closer to my goal?

Don't forget!

✅ **Check**
Did I complete yesterday's tasks?

⌗ **Focus**

Which of my core values do I want to focus on today?

What is important today?

🌀 **Weekly Reflection**

What negative thoughts or feelings (fear, envy, anger, etc.) accompanied me?

How can I accept them without letting them take over?

How do I feel today? ☹ ● ● ● ● ● ● ● ☺

👁 Mindfulness

I am **grateful and happy** because ...

....

....

....

♟ Mindset

Today is going to be **meaningful** because ...

....

....

⊕ Inner Strength

I am **determined** because ...

....

....

....

🎁 Good Deeds

What can I do for myself today?

....

....

What can I do for others today?

....

....

☀ Successes, Pleasures & Opportunities

....

....

....

⏱ Weekly Reflection

How much time have I spent on unnecessary distractions?

....

....

....

How can I avoid these distractions?

....

....

....

I'm working on this goal today

🔥 **Purpose & Motivation**

Imagine it with real, deep emotions!

How will I reward myself when I have reached my goal?

🚀 **Power**

✅ **Check**
Did I complete yesterday's tasks?

What will I do today in order to get closer to my goal?

☐
☐
☐

⟦⟧ **Focus**

What is important today?

Which of my core values do I want to focus on today?

🧭 **Weekly Reflection**

What stressed or annoyed me?

How can I avoid or improve this?

How do I feel today?   ☹ ● ● ● ● ● ● ● ☺

👁 Mindfulness

I am **grateful and happy** because ...

....

....

....

♛ Mindset

Today is going to be **brilliant** because ...

....

....

🎁 Good Deeds

What can I do for myself today?

....

....

What can I do for others today?

....

....

☀ Successes, Pleasures & Opportunities

Do you always write something down here? Think of little things too!

....

....

....

✒ Weekly Reflection

How often have I actually done the tasks I have planned?

....

....

....

How can I improve?

....

....

....

15

I'm working on this goal today ◎

🔥 Purpose & Motivation

What are the consequences if I don't reach my goal?

🚀 Power

What will I do today in order to get closer to my goal?

☐
☐
☐

☑ Check
Did I complete yesterday's tasks?

⟦⟧ Focus

Which of my core values do I want to focus on today?

What is important today?

You can also write a second goal here.

🧭 Weekly Reflection

What have I done for my own development?

What can I do for my development in the next 7 days?

How do I feel today? ● ● ● ● ● ● ●

👁 Mindfulness

I am **grateful and happy** because ...

....

....

....

➕ Inner Strength

I am **optimistic** because ...

....

....

....

👑 Mindset

Today is going to be **really good** because ...

....

....

In addition, you could write your feeling as a word here (see Reflection questions on pages 265 and 275).

🎁 Good Deeds

What can I do for myself today?

....

....

What can I do for others today?

....

....

☀ Successes, Pleasures & Opportunities

....

....

....

🧭 Weekly Reflection

In which situations have I behaved unfavorably?

....

....

....

What should I do instead?

....

....

....

DO THE MOST

1MPORTANT

THING

F1RST

" Things which matter most must never be at the mercy of things which matter least.

— Johann Wolfgang von Goethe

I'm working on this goal today

🔥 Purpose & Motivation

Why do I want to reach this goal?

🚀 Power

These things are really important! Make sure you do them!

✅ **Check**
Did I complete yesterday's tasks?

What will I do today in order to get closer to my goal?

☐
☐
☐

⟦⟧ Focus

Which of my core values do I want to focus on today?

What is important today?

🧭 Weekly Reflection

What robbed me of energy or did me no good?

How can I improve this?

How do I feel today? ☹ ● ● ● ● ● ● ● ☺

👁 Mindfulness

I am **grateful and happy** because ...

....

....

....

✚ Inner Strength

I am **successful** because ...

....

....

....

♛ Mindset

Today is going to be **wonderful** because ...

....

....

🎁 Good Deeds

What can I do for myself today?

....

....

What can I do for others today?

....

....

☀ Successes, Pleasures & Opportunities

....

....

....

⏱ Weekly Reflection

What self-critical beliefs did I notice?

....

....

....

What positive beliefs will I replace them with?

....

....

....

I'm working on this goal today

◎ **Purpose & Motivation**

Who or what
can support
me on the way
to my goal?

🚀 **Power**

What will I do
today in order
to get closer
to my goal?

☐
☐
☐

✅ **Check**
Did I complete
yesterday's tasks?

⌗ **Focus**

Which of my core values do I want
to focus on today?

What is important today?

*Note these in your
calendar or agenda!*

🧭 **Weekly Reflection**

❝ Challenge: Did I actually do the tasks
I planned and how did it feel?

❝ Challenge: What new or unusual actions
am I going to take in the next 14 days?

How do I feel today? ☹ ● ● ● ● ● ● ● ☺

👁 Mindfulness

I am **grateful and happy** because ...

_____

_____

_____

➕ Inner Strength

I am **competent** because ...

_____

_____

_____

👑 Mindset

Today is going to be **excellent** because ...

_____

_____

🎁 Good Deeds

It's best to write it down again, if you didn't do it.

What can I do for myself today? ◀┈┈▶ What can I do for others today?

_____   _____

_____   _____

☀ Successes, Pleasures & Opportunities

_____

_____

_____

🧭 Weekly Reflection

How well did I take care of myself?   Do I need to make any improvements?

_____   _____

_____   _____

_____   _____

> **I'm working on this goal today**
> ◎

🔥 **Purpose & Motivation**

What is going to be better when I have reached my goal?

🚀 **Power**

What will I do today in order to get closer to my goal?

☐
☐
☐

✅ **Check**
Did I complete yesterday's tasks?

⌖ **Focus**

Which of my core values do I want to focus on today?

What is important today?

🧭 **Weekly Reflection**

What was particularly good or gave me pleasure?

How can I cultivate this even more in my life?

How do I feel today? ● ● ● ● ● ● ●

👁 Mindfulness

I am **grateful and happy** because ...

....

....

....

⊕ Inner Strength

I am **strong** because ...

....

....

....

♛ Mindset

Today is going to be **very special** because ...

....

....

....

🎁 Good Deeds

What can I do for myself today?

....

....

What can I do for others today?

....

....

☀ Successes, Pleasures & Opportunities

....

....

....

If you take 100% responsibility for your experience, you have your destiny in your own hands!

🧭 Weekly Reflection

When have I felt like a victim or blamed others?

....

....

....

How am I going to handle this better?

....

....

....

I'm working on this goal today ◎

🔥 **Purpose & Motivation**

How will I feel when I have reached my goal?

🚀 **Power**

What will I do today in order to get closer to my goal?

☐
☐
☐

✅ **Check**
Did I complete yesterday's tasks?

⟦⟧ **Focus**

Which of my core values do I want to focus on today?

What is important today?

You can set a reminder for this on your phone.

✒ **Weekly Reflection**

How consistently have I worked on habit(s) in the last 7 days?

Which habit(s) do I want to focus on in the next 14 days?

How do I feel today? 😞 ● ● ● ● ● ● ○ ☺

Go for it!

👁 Mindfulness

I am **grateful and happy** because ...

....

....

....

♛ Mindset

Today is going to be **superb** because ...

....

....

🎁 Good Deeds

What can I do for myself today?

....

....

☀ Successes, Pleasures & Opportunities

....

....

....

➌ Inner Strength

I am **proud** because ...

....

....

....

What can I do for others today?

....

....

✏ Weekly Reflection

How satisfied am I with myself?

....

....

....

What can I do in the next 14 days to be fully satisfied with myself?

....

....

....

20

I'm working on this goal today

🔥 Purpose & Motivation

Who else will benefit when I reach my goal?

🚀 Power

What will I do today in order to get closer to my goal?

☐
☐
☐

✅ Check
Did I complete yesterday's tasks?

⚙ Focus

Which of my core values do I want to focus on today?

What is important today?

Try working with your power questions in these situations (see page 31).

❷ Weekly Reflection

What negative thoughts or feelings (fear, envy, anger, etc.) accompanied me?

How can I accept them without letting them take over?

How do I feel today? ○ ● ● ● ● ● ●

👁 Mindfulness

I am **grateful and happy** because ...

....

....

....

➕ Inner Strength

I am **determined** because ...

....

....

....

👑 Mindset

Today is going to be **meaningful** because ...

....

....

....

🎁 Good Deeds

What can I do for myself today?

....

....

What can I do for others today?

....

....

☀ Successes, Pleasures & Opportunities

....

....

....

🌑 Weekly Reflection

How much time have I spent on unnecessary distractions?

....

....

....

How can I avoid these distractions?

....

....

....

I'm working on this goal today

🔥 **Purpose & Motivation**

How will I reward myself when I have reached my goal?

🚀 **Power**

What will I do today in order to get closer to my goal?

☐

☐

☐

✅ **Check**
Did I complete yesterday's tasks?

⛶ **Focus**

Which of my core values do I want to focus on today?

What is important today?

🧭 **Weekly Reflection**

What stressed or annoyed me?

How can I avoid or improve this?

● ● ● ● ● ● ●

👁 Mindfulness

I am **grateful and happy** because …

....

....

....

👑 Mindset

Today is going to be **brilliant** because …

....

....

🎁 Good Deeds

What can I do for myself today?

....

....

⊕ Inner Strength

I am **persevering** because …

....

....

Don't be afraid to praise yourself!

What can I do for others today?

....

....

☀ Successes, Pleasures & Opportunities

....

....

....

🕐 Weekly Reflection

How often have I actually done the tasks I have planned?

....

....

....

How can I improve?

....

....

....

I'm working on this goal today

🔥 Purpose & Motivation

What are the consequences if I don't reach my goal?

🚀 Power

✅ Check
Did I complete yesterday's tasks?

What will I do today in order to get closer to my goal?

☐
☐
☐

⛶ Focus

What is important today?

Which of my core values do I want to focus on today?

🕒 Weekly Reflection

What have I done for my own development?

What can I do for my personal development in the near future?

How do I feel today? ● ● ● ● ● ● ●

👁 Mindfulness

I am **grateful and happy** because ...

....

....

....

♔ Mindset

Today is going to be **really good** because ...

....

....

🎁 Good Deeds

What can I do for myself today?

....

....

➕ Inner Strength

I am **optimistic** because ...

....

....

....

Not every day is perfect, but you can always start with a good attitude!

What can I do for others today?

....

....

☀ Successes, Pleasures & Opportunities

....

....

....

⚡ Weekly Reflection

In which situations have I behaved unfavorably?

....

....

....

What should I do instead?

....

....

....

EN J♥Y THE PROCESS

> There are only two mistakes one can make along the road to truth: not going all the way, and not starting.
>
> — Buddha

I'm working on this goal today

🔥 **Purpose & Motivation**

Why do I want to reach this goal?

🚀 **Power**

What will I do today in order to get closer to my goal?

☐
☐
☐

✅ **Check**
Did I complete yesterday's tasks?

⌗ **Focus**

Which of my core values do I want to focus on today?

What is important today?

Did you define these and write them down on pages 26-27?

❷ **Monthly Reflection**

What do I want most right now?

What will I do to get it?

How do I feel today? ● ● ● ● ● ● ●

👁 Mindfulness

I am **grateful and happy** because ...

_____

_____

_____

♟ Mindset

Today is going to be **wonderful** because ...

_____

_____

🎁 Good Deeds

What can I do for myself today?

_____

_____

☀ Successes, Pleasures & Opportunities

_____

_____

_____

➕ Inner Strength

I am **successful** because ...

_____

_____

_____

What can I do for others today?

_____

_____

🧭 Monthly Reflection

How have the last few weeks been?

_____

_____

_____

How do I want the next weeks to be and what do I need to do?

_____

_____

_____

I'm working
on this goal
today

🔥 Purpose & Motivation

Who or what
can support
me on the way
to my goal?

✈ Power

☐

☐

☐

✔ Check
Did I complete
yesterday's tasks?

What will I do
today in order
to get closer
to my goal?

[] Focus

Which of my core values do I want
to focus on today?

What is important today?

🕐 Monthly Reflection

How satisfied am I with my physical
condition?

Do I have to change anything?
What is it? How can I do it?

How do I feel today? ☹ ● ● ● ● ● ● ☺

👁 Mindfulness

I am **grateful and happy** because ...

➕ Inner Strength

I am **competent** because ...

♛ Mindset

Today is going to be **excellent** because ...

🎁 Good Deeds

What can I do for myself today?

What can I do for others today?

☀ Successes, Pleasures & Opportunities

..... *It makes you happier to write down positive things!*

🧭 Monthly Reflection

How satisfied am I with my mental state?

Do I have to change anything?
What is it? And how can I do it?

📅 **Day** »

I'm working on this goal today ◎

🔥 **Purpose & Motivation**

What is going to be better when I have reached the goal?

🚀 **Power**

What will I do today in order to get closer to my goal?

☑ **Check**
Did I complete yesterday's tasks?

☐
☐
☐

⟦⟧ **Focus**

Which of my core values do I want to focus on today?

What is important today?

Reminders in your cell phone are often a quick-and-easy fix for this.

✒ **Monthly Reflection**

How have I incorporated my core values that are important to me?

How can I integrate them even better into my life?

How do I feel today?   ● ● ● ● ● ● ●

👁 Mindfulness

I am **grateful and happy** because …

....

....

....

♔ Mindset

Today is going to be **very special** because …

....

....

🎁 Good Deeds

What can I do for myself today?

....

....

☀ Successes, Pleasures & Opportunities

....

....

....

⊕ Inner Strength

I am **strong** because …

....

....

....

What can I do for others today?

....

....

❽ Monthly Reflection

How have I progressed toward my goals?

....

....

....

What do I have to correct or how can I improve?

....

....

....

I'm working on this goal today ◎

🔥 **Purpose & Motivation**

How will I feel when I have reached my goal?

🚀 **Power**

☑ **Check**
Did I complete yesterday's tasks?

What will I do today in order to get closer to my goal?

☐
☐
☐

⟦ ⟧ **Focus**

Which of my core values do I want to focus on today?

What is important today?

🔅 **Monthly Reflection**

What was I particularly preoccupied with or worried about?

What can I do to change it or better deal with it?

👁 Mindfulness

I am **grateful and happy** because …

....

....

....

➕ Inner Strength

I am **proud** because …

....

....

....

♛ Mindset

Today is going to be **superb** because …

....

....

🎁 Good Deeds

What can I do for myself today?

....

....

What can I do for others today?

....

....

☀ Successes, Pleasures & Opportunities

....

....

....

Schedule this right away!

🧭 Monthly Reflection

How much joy, fun, and free time for great experiences were there in the last weeks?

....

....

....

How can I consciously integrate them into my life in the next few weeks?

....

....

....

I'm working on this goal today

◎ _____

🔥 **Purpose & Motivation**

Who else will profit when I reach my goal?

🚀 **Power**

☐ ✅ **Check**
Did I complete yesterday's tasks?

What will I do today in order to get closer to my goal?

☐

☐

⟦ ⟧ **Focus**

Which of my core values do I want to focus on today?

What is important today?

It's best to do the most important things first!

🎯 **Monthly Reflection**

How consistently did I keep focus on the important things?

How can I spend more time with important things?

👁 Mindfulness

I am **grateful and happy** because ...

....

....

....

♛ Mindset

Today is going to be **meaningful** because ...

....

....

🎁 Good Deeds

What can I do for myself today?

....

....

☀ Successes, Pleasures & Opportunities

....

....

....

➕ Inner Strength

I am **determined** because ...

....

....

....

What can I do for others today?

....

....

🧭 Monthly Reflection

Where did I use excuses not to do something I planned to do?

....

....

....

What can I do to improve in the future?

....

....

....

I'm working on this goal today

🔥 **Purpose & Motivation**

You can also use this for a visualization.

How will I reward myself when I have reached my goal?

🚀 **Power**

☑ **Check**
Did I complete yesterday's tasks?

What will I do today in order to get closer to my goal?

☐
☐
☐

⟦⟧ **Focus**

Which of my core values do I want to focus on today?

What is important today?

🧭 **Monthly Reflection**

What was my biggest challenge in the last few weeks?

What could I have done better?

👁 Mindfulness

I am **grateful and happy** because …

....

....

....

➕ Inner Strength

I am **persevering** because …

....

....

....

♛ Mindset

Today is going to be **brilliant** because …

....

....

🎁 Good Deeds

What can I do for myself today?

....

....

What can I do for others today?

....

....

☀ Successes, Pleasures & Opportunities

....

....

....

🕐 Monthly Reflection

How satisfied am I with myself and my personal development?

....

....

....

Do I have to change anything?
What is it? And how can I do it?

....

....

....

I'm working on this goal today

◎

🔥 Purpose & Motivation

What are the consequences if I don't reach the goal?

🚀 Power

What will I do today in order to get closer to my goal?

☐
☐
☐

✅ **Check**
Did I complete yesterday's tasks?

⟦⟧ Focus

Which of my core values do I want to focus on today?

What is important today?

Create your wheel of life (see pages 36-37) if you haven't done so yet.

🕐 Monthly Reflection

In which areas of my life do I currently have shortcomings?

Do I want or have to live with them? What can I do to improve?

👁 Mindfulness

I am **grateful and happy** because …

_____

_____

_____

♛ Mindset

Today is going to be **really good** because …

_____

_____

🎁 Good Deeds

What can I do for myself today?

_____

_____

What can I do for others today?

_____

_____

☀ Successes, Pleasures & Opportunities

_____

_____

_____

⊕ Inner Strength

I am **optimistic** because …

_____

_____

_____

🧭 Monthly Reflection

What dreams do I have that I would like to fulfill in the near future?

_____

_____

_____

How and when will I implement them?

_____

_____

_____

> Let him who would move the world first move himself.
> — Socrates

I'm working on this goal today

🔥 **Purpose & Motivation**

You need to have a precise answer to the "why"; if not, something does not fit!

Why do I want to reach this goal?

🚀 **Power**

What will I do today in order to get closer to my goal?

☑ **Check**
Did I complete yesterday's tasks?

☐
☐
☐

⟦ ⟧ **Focus**

Which of my core values do I want to focus on today?

What is important today?

📍 **Weekly Reflection**

What robbed me of energy or did me no good?

How can I improve this?

👁 Mindfulness

I am **grateful and happy** because ...

....

....

....

➕ Inner Strength

I am **successful** because ...

....

....

....

👑 Mindset

Today is going to be **wonderful** because ...

....

....

....

🎁 Good Deeds

What can I do for myself today?

....

....

What can I do for others today?

....

....

☀ Successes, Pleasures & Opportunities

....

....

....

🧭 Weekly Reflection

What self-critical beliefs did I notice?

....

....

....

What positive beliefs will I replace them with?

....

....

....

I'm working on this goal today

🔥 **Purpose & Motivation**

Who or what can support me on the way to my goal?

🚀 **Power**

What will I do today in order to get closer to my goal?

☑ **Check**
Did I complete yesterday's tasks?

▢
▢
▢

[ ] **Focus**

Which of my core values do I want to focus on today?

What is important today?

Dress completely different, visit an unknown place, or read a book in another language ...

🧭 **Weekly Reflection**

CC Challenge: Did I actually do the tasks I planned and how did it feel?

CC Challenge: What new or unusual actions am I going to take in the next 7 days?

👁 Mindfulness

I am **grateful and happy** because ...

➕ Inner Strength

I am **competent** because ...

👑 Mindset

Today is going to be **excellent** because ...

Don't put too much pressure on yourself and think of little things too!

🎁 Good Deeds

What can I do for myself today?

What can I do for others today?

☀ Successes, Pleasures & Opportunities

🧭 Weekly Reflection

How well did I take care of myself?

Do I need to make any improvements?

I'm working on this goal today

🔥 **Purpose & Motivation**

What is going to be better when I have reached my goal?

🚀 **Power**

What will I do today in order to get closer to my goal?

☑ **Check**
Did I complete yesterday's tasks?

☐

☐

☐

⟦ ⟧ **Focus**

Which of my core values do I want to focus on today?

What is important today?

🧭 **Weekly Reflection**

What was particularly good or gave me pleasure?

How can I cultivate this even more in my life?

How do I feel today? ☹ ● ● ● ● ● ● ● ☺

👁 Mindfulness

I am **grateful and happy** because ...

....

....

....

➕ Inner Strength

I am **strong** because ...

....

....

....

👑 Mindset

Today is going to be **very special** because ...

....

....

Conscious gratitude makes your life richer every day!

🎁 Good Deeds

What can I do for myself today?

....

....

What can I do for others today?

....

....

☀ Successes, Pleasures & Opportunities

....

....

....

❷ Weekly Reflection

When have I felt like a victim or blamed others?

....

....

....

How am I going to handle this better?

....

....

....

I'm working on this goal today

🔥 **Purpose & Motivation**

How will I feel when I have reached my goal?

🚀 **Power**

What will I do today in order to get closer to my goal?

☑ **Check**
Did I complete yesterday's tasks?

⌂ **Focus**

Which of my core values do I want to focus on today?

What is important today?

🧭 **Weekly Reflection**

Do you drink enough water?

How consistently have I been working on habits over the last 14 days?

Which habit(s) do I want to work on in the next 7 days?

How do I feel today? ☹ ● ● ● ● ● ● ● ☺

👁 Mindfulness

I am **grateful and happy** because ...

➕ Inner Strength

I am **proud** because ...

♛ Mindset

Today is going to be **superb** because ...

🎁 Good Deeds

What can I do for myself today?

What can I do for others today?

☀ Successes, Pleasures & Opportunities

🧭 Weekly Reflection

How satisfied am I with myself?

What can I do in the next 7 days to be fully satisfied with myself?

I'm working on this goal today ◎

Do you have strong visual images for your goals?

🔥 **Purpose & Motivation**

Who else will benefit when I reach my goal?

🚀 **Power**

What will I do today in order to get closer to my goal?

☐
☐
☐

✅ **Check**
Did I complete yesterday's tasks?

⛶ **Focus**

Which of my core values do I want to focus on today?

What is important today?

🧭 **Weekly Reflection**

What negative thoughts or feelings (fear, envy, anger, etc.) accompanied me?

How can I accept them without letting them take over?

How do I feel today?   ● ● ● ● ● ● ●

👁 Mindfulness

I am **grateful and happy** because ...

➕ Inner Strength

I am **determined** because ...

♛ Mindset

Today is going to be **meaningful** because ...

🎁 Good Deeds

What can I do for myself today?

What can I do for others today?

☀ Successes, Pleasures & Opportunities

🧭 Weekly Reflection

How much time have I spent on unnecessary distractions?

How can I avoid these distractions?

I'm working on this goal today ◎

🔥 **Purpose & Motivation**

How will I reward myself when I have reached my goal?

🚀 **Power**

☑ **Check**
Did I complete yesterday's tasks?

What will I do today in order to get closer to my goal?

☐

☐

☐

⟦⟧ **Focus**

What is important today?

Which of my core values do I want to focus on today?

🧭 **Weekly Reflection**

What stressed or annoyed me?

How can I avoid or improve this?

How do I feel today? ☹ ● ● ● ● ● ● ● ☺

👁 Mindfulness

I am **grateful and happy** because ...

....

....

....

♛ Mindset

Today is going to be **brilliant** because ...

....

....

🎁 Good Deeds

What do you do for others without noticing anymore?

What can I do for myself today?

....

....

What can I do for others today?

....

....

☀ Successes, Pleasures & Opportunities

....

....

....

....

➕ Inner Strength

I am **persevering** because ...

....

....

....

🧭 Weekly Reflection

How often have I actually done the tasks I have planned?

....

....

....

How can I improve?

....

....

....

I'm working on this goal today

🔥 Purpose & Motivation

What are the consequences if I don't reach my goal?

🚀 Power

What will I do today in order to get closer to my goal?

☐
☐
☐

✅ Check
Did I complete yesterday's tasks?

⟦ ⟧ Focus

Which of my core values do I want to focus on today?

What is important today?

Have you tried listening to audio books and podcasts?

🧭 Weekly Reflection

What have I done for my own development?

What can I do for my development in the next 7 days?

How do I feel today?   ● ● ● ● ● ● ●   ☺

👁 Mindfulness

I am **grateful and happy** because ...

....

....

....

⊕ Inner Strength

I am **optimistic** because ...

....

....

....

👑 Mindset

Today is going to be **really good** because ...

....

....

🎁 Good Deeds

What can I do for myself today?

....

....

What can I do for others today?

....

....

☀ Successes, Pleasures & Opportunities

....

....

....

✦ Weekly Reflection

In which situations have I behaved unfavorably?

....

....

....

What should I do instead?

....

....

....

NOT PERFECT

→ BUT ←

ON THE
PATH

❝ The highest reward for a person's toil is not what they get for it, but what they become by it.

— John Ruskin

I'm working on this goal today

🔥 **Purpose & Motivation**

Why do I want to reach this goal?

🚀 **Power**

What will I do today in order to get closer to my goal?

☑ **Check**
Did I complete yesterday's tasks?

⌗ **Focus**

Which of my core values do I want to focus on today?

What is important today?

🧭 **Weekly Reflection**

What robbed me of energy or did me no good?

How can I improve this?

👁 Mindfulness

I am **grateful and happy** because ...

⊕ Inner Strength

I am **successful** because ...

♛ Mindset

Today is going to be **wonderful** because ...

🎁 Good Deeds

What can I do for myself today?

Sometimes a simple compliment is enough—even one for yourself!

What can I do for others today?

☀ Successes, Pleasures & Opportunities

⚊ Weekly Reflection

What self-critical beliefs did I notice?

What positive beliefs will I replace them with?

I'm working on this goal today

🔥 **Purpose & Motivation**

Use all the support you can get! Ask others for ideas!

Who or what can support me on the way to my goal?

🚀 **Power**

☑ **Check**
Did I complete yesterday's tasks?

What will I do today in order to get closer to my goal?

☐
☐
☐

⟦ ⟧ **Focus**

Which of my core values do I want to focus on today?

What is important today?

Stay flexible and don't overburden yourself with it!

❽ **Weekly Reflection**

❝❝ Challenge: Did I actually do the tasks I planned and how did it feel?

❝❝ Challenge: What new or unusual actions am I going to take in the next 7 days?

👁 Mindfulness

I am **grateful and happy** because ...

....

....

....

👑 Mindset

Today is going to be **excellent** because ...

....

....

🎁 Good Deeds

What can I do for myself today?

....

....

What can I do for others today?

....

....

☀ Successes, Pleasures & Opportunities

....

....

....

🧭 Weekly Reflection

How well did I take care of myself?

....

....

....

Do I need to make any improvements?

....

....

....

📅 **Day** »

I'm working on this goal today ◎

🔥 **Purpose & Motivation**

What is going to
be better when
I have reached
my goal?

🚀 **Power**

What will I do
today in order
to get closer
to my goal?

☑ **Check**
Did I complete
yesterday's tasks?

⟦⟧ **Focus**

Which of my core values do I want
to focus on today?

What is important today?

🧭 **Weekly Reflection**

What was particularly good or gave me
pleasure?

How can I cultivate this even more in
my life?

How do I feel today? ● ● ● ● ● ● ●

👁 Mindfulness

I am **grateful and happy** because ...

....

....

....

⊕ Inner Strength

I am **strong** because ...

....

....

....

♛ Mindset

Today is going to be **very special** because ...

....

....

....

🎁 Good Deeds

What can I do for myself today?

....

....

What can I do for others today?

....

....

☼ Successes, Pleasures & Opportunities

....

....

....

⚡ Weekly Reflection

When have I felt like a victim or blamed others?

....

....

....

How am I going to handle this better?

....

....

....

I'm working on this goal today

🔥 Purpose & Motivation

How will I feel when I have reached my goal?

🚀 Power

What will I do today in order to get closer to my goal?

☑ **Check**
Did I complete yesterday's tasks?

☐
☐
☐

⟦ ⟧ Focus

Which of my core values do I want to focus on today?

What is important today?

🧭 Weekly Reflection

Have you exercised enough?

How consistently have I worked on habit(s) in the last 7 days?

Which habit(s) do I want to work on in the next 7 days?

How do I feel today?   ● ● ● ● ● ● ●

👁 Mindfulness

I am **grateful and happy** because ...

....

....

....

➕ Inner Strength

I am **proud** because ...

....

....

....

👑 Mindset

Today is going to be **superb** because ...

....

....

🎁 Good Deeds

What can I do for myself today?

....

....

What can I do for others today?

....

....

☀ Successes, Pleasures & Opportunities

....

....

....

🧭 Weekly Reflection

How satisfied am I with myself?

....

....

....

What can I do in the next 7 days to be fully satisfied with myself?

....

....

....

I'm working on this goal today

🔥 **Purpose & Motivation**

Who else will benefit when I reach my goal?

🚀 **Power**

✅ **Check**
Did I complete yesterday's tasks?

What will I do today in order to get closer to my goal?

☐
☐
☐

⟦⟧ **Focus**

Which of my core values do I want to focus on today?

What is important today?

🍂 **Weekly Reflection**

What negative thoughts or feelings (fear, envy, anger, etc.) accompanied me?

How can I accept them without letting them take over?

How do I feel today? ☹ ● ● ● ● ● ● ● ☺

👁 Mindfulness

I am **grateful and happy** because ...

....

....

....

➕ Inner Strength

I am **determined** because ...

....

....

....

♛ Mindset

Today is going to be **meaningful** because ...

....

....

🎁 Good Deeds

What can I do for myself today?

....

....

What can I do for others today?

....

....

☀ Successes, Pleasures & Opportunities

....

....

....

✒ Weekly Reflection

How much time have I spent on unnecessary distractions?

....

....

....

How can I avoid these distractions?

....

....

....

I'm working on this goal today

🔥 Purpose & Motivation

How will I reward myself when I have reached my goal?

🚀 **Power**

Do you really always do this?

☑️ **Check**
Did I complete yesterday's tasks?

What will I do today in order to get closer to my goal?

- ☐
- ☐
- ☐

⟦ ⟧ **Focus**

Which of my core values do I want to focus on today?

What is important today?

🧭 Weekly Reflection

What stressed or annoyed me?

How can I avoid or improve this?

How do I feel today? ☹ ● ● ● ● ● ● ● ☺

👁 Mindfulness

I am **grateful and happy** because …

....

....

....

✚ Inner Strength

I am **persevering** because …

....

....

....

♕ Mindset

Today is going to be **brilliant** because …

....

....

🎁 Good Deeds

What can I do for myself today?

....

....

What can I do for others today?

....

....

☀ Successes, Pleasures & Opportunities

....

....

....

🕑 Weekly Reflection

How often have I actually done the tasks I have planned?

....

....

....

How can I improve?

....

....

....

I'm working on this goal today ⊙

🔥 Purpose & Motivation

What are the consequences if I don't reach my goal?

🚀 Power

What will I do today in order to get closer to my goal?

☐
☐
☐

✅ Check
Did I complete yesterday's tasks?

⌨ Focus

Which of my core values do I want to focus on today?

What is important today?

🧭 Weekly Reflection

What have I done for my own development?

What can I do for my personal development in the near future?

How do I feel today? ☹ ● ● ● ● ● ● ● ☺

👁 Mindfulness

I am **grateful and happy** because ...

....
....
....

♟ Mindset

Today is going to be **really good** because ...

....
....

🎁 Good Deeds

What can I do for myself today?

....
....

What can I do for others today?

....
....

☀ Successes, Pleasures & Opportunities

....
....
....

➋ Weekly Reflection

In which situations have I behaved unfavorably?

....
....
....

What should I do instead?

....
....
....

➕ Inner Strength

I am **optimistic** because ...

....
....
....

147

BE

FRIENDLY

AND START WITH

YOURSELF

NOOM: 3/15/21 EMOTIONS

1. HAPPY
2. EXCITED
3. FRUSTRATED
4. BOARED
5.

Peace comes from within. Do not seek it without.
— Buddha

I'm working on this goal today

🔥 **Purpose & Motivation**

Why do I want to reach this goal?

🚀 **Power**

What will I do today in order to get closer to my goal?

☑ **Check**
Did I complete yesterday's tasks?

⟦ ⟧ **Focus**

Which of my core values do I want to focus on today?

What is important today?

✒ **Weekly Reflection**

What robbed me of energy or did me no good?

How can I improve this?

How do I feel today?   ☹ ● ● ● ● ● ● ● ☺

👁 Mindfulness

I am **grateful and happy** because ...

....

....

....

⊕ Inner Strength

I am **successful** because ...

....

....

....

♛ Mindset

Today is going to be **wonderful** because ...

....

....

...... Don't forget yourself!

🎁 Good Deeds

What can I do for myself today?

....

....

What can I do for others today?

....

....

☀ Successes, Pleasures & Opportunities

....

....

....

⏱ Weekly Reflection

What self-critical beliefs did I notice?

....

....

....

What positive beliefs will I replace them with?

....

....

....

I'm working on this goal today

◉

🔥 Purpose & Motivation

Who or what can support me on the way to my goal?

🚀 Power

☐

☐

☐

☑ **Check**
Did I complete yesterday's tasks?

What will I do today in order to get closer to my goal?

⟦⟧ Focus

Which of my core values do I want to focus on today?

What is important today?

🧭 Weekly Reflection

❝❝ Challenge: Did I actually do the tasks I planned and how did it feel?

❝❝ Challenge: What new or unusual actions am I going to take in the next 14 days?

👁 Mindfulness

I am **grateful and happy** because ...

➕ Inner Strength

I am **competent** because ...

👑 Mindset

Today is going to be **excellent** because ...

Do you often not fill out everything? Stay alert and don't get too comfortable!

🎁 Good Deeds

What can I do for myself today?

What can I do for others today?

☀ Successes, Pleasures & Opportunities

🕑 Weekly Reflection

How well did I take care of myself?

Do I need to make any improvements?

I'm working on this goal today

🔥 **Purpose & Motivation**

Consider all the positive aspects that reaching your goal entails!

What is going to be better when I have reached my goal?

🚀 **Power**

What will I do today in order to get closer to my goal?

☐
☐
☐

✅ **Check**
Did I complete yesterday's tasks?

⟦⟧ **Focus**

Which of my core values do I want to focus on today?

What is important today?

🧭 **Weekly Reflection**

What was particularly good or gave me pleasure?

How can I cultivate this even more in my life?

How do I feel today?   ● ● ● ● ● ● ●

👁 Mindfulness

I am **grateful and happy** because ...

....

....

....

➕ Inner Strength

I am **strong** because ...

....

....

....

👑 Mindset

Today is going to be **very special** because ...

....

....

🎁 Good Deeds

What can I do for myself today?

....

....

What can I do for others today?

....

....

☀ Successes, Pleasures & Opportunities

....

....

....

🧭 Weekly Reflection

When have I felt like a victim or blamed others?

....

....

....

How am I going to handle this better?

....

....

....

📅 **Day** »

47

I'm working on this goal today

🔥 **Purpose & Motivation**

How will I feel when I have reached my goal?

🚀 **Power**

What will I do today in order to get closer to my goal?

☑ **Check**
Did I complete yesterday's tasks?

⬚

⬚

⬚

⟦ ⟧ **Focus**

Which of my core values do I want to focus on today?

What is important today?

🍂 **Weekly Reflection**

How consistently have I worked on habit(s) in the last 7 days?

Which habit(s) do I want to focus on in the next 14 days?

How do I feel today?   ☹ ● ● ● ● ● ● ● ☺

👁 Mindfulness

I am **grateful and happy** because ...

....

....

....

✚ Inner Strength

I am **proud** because ...

....

....

....

♛ Mindset

Today is going to be **superb** because ...

....

....

🎁 Good Deeds

What can I do for myself today?

....

....

What can I do for others today?

....

....

☀ Successes, Pleasures & Opportunities

....

....

....

🧭 Weekly Reflection

How satisfied am I with myself?

....

....

....

What can I do in the next 14 days to be as satisfied with myself as possible?

....

....

....

I'm working on this goal today ◎

🔥 **Purpose & Motivation**

Who else will benefit when I reach my goal?

🚀 **Power**

What will I do today in order to get closer to my goal?

☐
☐
☐

✅ **Check**
Did I complete yesterday's tasks?

⌐⌐ **Focus**

Which of my core values do I want to focus on today?

What is important today?

🧭 **Weekly Reflection**

What negative thoughts or feelings (fear, envy, anger, etc.) accompanied me?

How can I accept them without letting them take over?

How do I feel today? ● ● ● ● ● ● ●

👁 Mindfulness

I am **grateful and happy** because ...

....

....

....

➕ Inner Strength

I am **determined** because ...

....

....

....

👑 Mindset

Today is going to be **meaningful** because ...

....

....

....

🎁 Good Deeds

What can I do for myself today?

....

....

What can I do for others today?

....

....

☼ Successes, Pleasures & Opportunities

....

....

....

Do you know the 60/60/30 method? 60 minutes of fully concentrated work, a 5-minute break, another 60 minutes of concentration, and then 30 minutes of relaxation.

🧭 Weekly Reflection

How much time have I spent on unnecessary distractions?

....

....

....

How can I avoid these distractions?

....

....

....

I'm working on this goal today ◎

🔥 Purpose & Motivation

How will I reward myself when I have reached my goal?

🚀 Power

What will I do today in order to get closer to my goal?

☐
☐
☐

✅ Check
Did I complete yesterday's tasks?

[ ] Focus

Which of my core values do I want to focus on today?

What is important today?

⚡ Weekly Reflection

What stressed or annoyed me?

How can I avoid or improve this?

👁 Mindfulness

I am **grateful and happy** because ...

....

....

....

➕ Inner Strength

I am **persevering** because ...

....

....

....

♛ Mindset

Today is going to be **brilliant** because ...

....

....

🎁 Good Deeds

What can I do for myself today?

....

....

What can I do for others today?

....

....

☀ Successes, Pleasures & Opportunities

....

....

....

⏱ Weekly Reflection

How often have I actually done the tasks
I have planned?

....

....

....

How can I improve?

....

....

....

I'm working
on this goal
today

🔥 Purpose & Motivation

What are the
consequences
if I don't reach
my goal?

🚀 Power

What will I do
today in order
to get closer
to my goal?

☑ **Check**
Did I complete
yesterday's tasks?

☐

☐

☐

🔲 Focus

Which of my core values do I want
to focus on today?

What is important today?

✒ Weekly Reflection

What have I done for my own
development?

What can I do for my personal
development in the next 14 days?

How do I feel today?   ● ● ● ● ● ● ●

👁 Mindfulness

I am **grateful and happy** because ...

....

....

....

➕ Inner Strength

I am **optimistic** because ...

....

....

....

👑 Mindset

Today is going to be **really good** because ...

....

....

🎁 Good Deeds

What can I do for myself today?

....

....

What can I do for others today?

....

....

☀ Successes, Pleasures & Opportunities

....

....

....

🖊 Weekly Reflection

In which situations have I behaved unfavorably?

....

....

....

What should I do instead?

....

....

....

My Beliefs

👎 **This is what I believed so far:** ....

....

👍 **I want to believe this instead:** ....

....

....

👎 **This is what I believed so far:** ....

....

👍 **I want to believe this instead:** ....

....

....

👎 **This is what I believed so far:** ....

....

👍 **I want to believe this instead:** ....

....

....

👎 **This is what I believed so far:** ....

....

👍 **I want to believe this instead:** ....

....

....

👎 This is what
I believed
so far:

....
....
....

👍 **I want to
believe this
instead:**

....
....
....

👎 This is what
I believed
so far:

....
....
....

👍 **I want to
believe this
instead:**

....
....
....

👎 This is what
I believed
so far:

....
....
....

👍 **I want to
believe this
instead:**

....
....
....

👎 This is what
I believed
so far:

....
....
....

👍 **I want to
believe this
instead:**

....
....
....

I'm working on this goal today

🔥 **Purpose & Motivation**

Why do I want to reach this goal?

🚀 **Power**

What will I do today in order to get closer to my goal?

☑ **Check**
Did I complete yesterday's tasks?

⌞⌝ **Focus**

Which of my core values do I want to focus on today?

What is important today?

🧭 **Monthly Reflection**

What do I want most right now?

What will I do to get it?

How do I feel today?   ● ● ● ● ● ● ●

👁 Mindfulness

I am **grateful and happy** because …

....

....

....

➕ Inner Strength

I am **successful** because …

....

....

....

♛ Mindset

Today is going to be **wonderful** because …

....

....

🎁 Good Deeds

What can I do for myself today?

....

....

What can I do for others today?

....

....

☀ Successes, Pleasures & Opportunities

....

....

....

🧭 Monthly Reflection

How have the last few weeks been?

....

....

....

How do I want the next weeks to be and what do I need to do?

....

....

....

I'm working on this goal today

◎

🔥 Purpose & Motivation

Who or what can support me on the way to my goal?

🚀 Power

What will I do today in order to get closer to my goal?

☐
☐
☐

✅ Check
Did I complete yesterday's tasks?

⟨⟩ Focus

Which of my core values do I want to focus on today?

What is important today?

🧭 Monthly Reflection

How satisfied am I with my physical condition?

Do I have to change anything? What is it? How can I do it?

How do I feel today? ○ ● ● ● ● ● ● ●

👁 Mindfulness

I am **grateful and happy** because ...

....

....

....

➕ Inner Strength

I am **competent** because ...

....

....

....

👑 Mindset

Today is going to be **excellent** because ...

....

....

🎁 Good Deeds

What can I do for myself today?

....

....

What can I do for others today?

....

....

☀ Successes, Pleasures & Opportunities

....

....

....

Do you have enough time for relaxation and peace of mind?

🏃 Monthly Reflection

How satisfied am I with my mental state?

....

....

....

Do I have to change anything? What is it? And how can I do it?

....

....

....

I'm working on this goal today

🔥 Purpose & Motivation

What is going to be better when I have reached the goal?

🚀 Power

What will I do today in order to get closer to my goal?

☐
☐
☐

✓ Check
Did I complete yesterday's tasks?

⟦ ⟧ Focus

Which of my core values do I want to focus on today?

What is important today?

🧭 Monthly Reflection

How have I incorporated my core values that are important to me?

How can I integrate them even better into my life?

How do I feel today?   ☹   ● ● ● ● ● ● ●   ☺

👁 Mindfulness

I am **grateful and happy** because ...

....

....

....

♟ Inner Strength

I am **strong** because ...

....

....

....

♛ Mindset

Today is going to be **very special** because ...

....

....

....

🎁 Good Deeds

What can I do for myself today?

....

....

What can I do for others today?

....

....

☀ Successes, Pleasures & Opportunities

....

....

....

Do you consistently implement your daily goal-oriented actions? ·······▶

❹ Monthly Reflection

How have I progressed toward my goals?

....

....

....

What do I have to correct or how can I improve?

....

....

....

54

I'm working
on this goal
today

🔥 **Purpose & Motivation**

Also think about what impact this will have on your feelings in the medium and long term!

How will I feel
when I have
reached my
goal?

🚀 **Power**

✅ **Check**
Did I complete
yesterday's tasks?

What will I do
today in order
to get closer
to my goal?

⟦⟧ **Focus**

What is important today?

Which of my core values do I want
to focus on today?

🧭 **Monthly Reflection**

What was I particularly preoccupied with
or worried about?

What can I do to change it or better
deal with it?

How do I feel today? ☹ ● ● ● ● ● ● ● ☺

👁 Mindfulness

I am **grateful and happy** because ...

➕ Inner Strength

I am **proud** because ...

👑 Mindset

Today is going to be **superb** because ...

🎁 Good Deeds

What can I do for myself today?

What can I do for others today?

☀ Successes, Pleasures & Opportunities

🧭 Monthly Reflection

How much joy, fun, and free time for great experiences were there in the last weeks?

How can I consciously integrate them into my life in the next few weeks?

I'm working on this goal today

🔥 **Purpose & Motivation**

Who else will profit when I reach my goal?

🚀 **Power**

What will I do today in order to get closer to my goal?

☐
☐
☐

✅ **Check**
Did I complete yesterday's tasks?

⟦⟧ **Focus**

Which of my core values do I want to focus on today?

What is important today?

🕐 **Monthly Reflection**

How consistently did I keep focus on the important things?

How can I spend more time with important things?

How do I feel today?   ● ● ● ● ● ● ●

👁 Mindfulness

I am **grateful and happy** because ...

....

....

....

➕ Inner Strength

I am **determined** because ...

....

....

....

♛ Mindset

Today is going to be **meaningful** because ...

....

....

🎁 Good Deeds

What can I do for myself today?

....

....

What can I do for others today?

....

....

☀ Successes, Pleasures & Opportunities

....

....

....

What would it be like if you commited to others ......
(include consequences for not following through)?

⏱ Monthly Reflection

Where did I use excuses not to do
something I planned to do?

....

....

....

What can I do to improve in the future?

....

....

....

56

I'm working on this goal today

🔥 Purpose & Motivation

How will I reward myself when I have reached my goal?

🚀 Power

What will I do today in order to get closer to my goal?

☐
☐
☐

✓ Check
Did I complete yesterday's tasks?

[ ] Focus

Which of my core values do I want to focus on today?

What is important today?

🧭 Monthly Reflection

What was my biggest challenge in the last few weeks?

What could I have done better?

How do I feel today? ☹ ● ● ● ● ● ● ●

👁 Mindfulness

I am **grateful and happy** because ...

....

....

....

➕ Inner Strength

I am **persevering** because ...

....

....

....

♛ Mindset

Today is going to be **brilliant** because ...

....

....

🎁 Good Deeds

What can I do for myself today?

....

....

What can I do for others today?

....

....

☀ Successes, Pleasures & Opportunities

....

....

....

🕐 Monthly Reflection

How satisfied am I with myself and my personal development?

....

....

....

Do I have to change anything?
What is it? And how can I do it?

....

....

....

I'm working on this goal today ◉

🔥 **Purpose & Motivation**

What are the consequences if I don't reach the goal?

🚀 **Power**

What will I do today in order to get closer to my goal?

☐
☐
☐

✅ **Check**
Did I complete yesterday's tasks?

⟦⟧ **Focus**

Which of my core values do I want to focus on today?

What is important today?

⏱ **Monthly Reflection**

In which areas of my life do I currently have shortcomings?

Do I want or have to live with them? What can I do to improve?

👁 Mindfulness

I am **grateful and happy** because ...

⊕ Inner Strength

I am **optimistic** because ...

♛ Mindset

Today is going to be **really good** because ...

🎁 Good Deeds

What can I do for myself today?

What can I do for others today?

☀ Successes, Pleasures & Opportunities

Have you written down any inspiring things on your wish list (see pages 38-39)?

❻ Monthly Reflection

What dreams do I have that I would like to fulfill in the near future?

How and when will I implement them?

YOUR
PATH
IS THE **GOAL**

GOAL GOAL GOAL GOAL GOAL GOAL GOAL GOAL GOAL GOAL GOAL GOAL GOAL GOAL GOAL

❝ Start by doing what's necessary, then do what's possible, and suddenly you are doing the impossible.

— Saint Francis of Assisi

I'm working on this goal today

🔥 **Purpose & Motivation**

Why do I want
to reach this
goal?

🚀 **Power**

✅ **Check**
Did I complete
yesterday's tasks?

What will I do
today in order
to get closer
to my goal?

☐
☐
☐

⟦⟧ **Focus**

Which of my core values do I want
to focus on today?

What is important today?

🧭 **Weekly Reflection**

What robbed me of energy or did me no
good?

How can I improve this?

● ● ● ● ● ● ●

👁 Mindfulness

I am **grateful and happy** because ...

....

....

....

♛ Mindset

Today is going to be **wonderful** because ...

....

....

🎁 Good Deeds

What can I do for myself today?

....

....

☀ Successes, Pleasures & Opportunities

....

....

....

⊕ Inner Strength

I am **successful** because ...

....

....

....

What can I do for others today?

....

....

Look at your new beliefs every now and then!

🕐 Weekly Reflection

What self-critical beliefs did I notice?

....

....

....

What positive beliefs will I replace them with?

....

....

....

I'm working on this goal today ⊙ ....
....
....

🔥 Purpose & Motivation

Who or what
can support
me on the way
to my goal? ....
....
....

🚀 Power

☑ **Check**
Did I complete
yesterday's tasks?

What will I do
today in order
to get closer
to my goal?

☐
☐
☐

[] Focus

Which of my core values do I want
to focus on today?

....
....

What is important today?

....
....
....

⚡ Weekly Reflection

Challenge: Did I actually do the tasks
I planned and how did it feel?

....
....
....

Challenge: What new or unusual actions
am I going to take in the next 7 days?

....
....
....

How do I feel today?   ● ● ● ● ● ● ●

👁 Mindfulness

I am **grateful and happy** because ...

....

....

....

➕ Inner Strength

I am **competent** because ...

....

....

....

👑 Mindset

Today is going to be **excellent** because ...

....

....

....

🎁 Good Deeds

What can I do for myself today?

....

....

What can I do for others today?

....

....

☀ Successes, Pleasures & Opportunities

....

....

....

⚡ Weekly Reflection

How well did I take care of myself?

....

....

....

Do I need to make any improvements?

....

....

....

I'm working on this goal today

🔥 Purpose & Motivation

What is going to be better when I have reached my goal?

🚀 Power

✅ **Check**
Did I complete yesterday's tasks?

What will I do today in order to get closer to my goal?

☐
☐
☐

⟦⟧ Focus

Which of my core values do I want to focus on today?

What is important today?

🧭 Weekly Reflection

What was particularly good or gave me pleasure?

How can I cultivate this even more in my life?

👁 Mindfulness

I am **grateful and happy** because …

....

....

....

⊕ Inner Strength

I am **strong** because …

....

....

....

♛ Mindset

Today is going to be **very special** because …

....

....

....

🎁 Good Deeds

What can I do for myself today?

....

....

What can I do for others today?

....

....

☀ Successes, Pleasures & Opportunities

....

....

....

This can help you to concentrate on your sphere of influence. ....

⚡ Weekly Reflection

When have I felt like a victim or blamed others?

....

....

....

How am I going to handle this better?

....

....

....

I'm working on this goal today

◉ **Purpose & Motivation**

How will I feel when I have reached my goal?

🚀 **Power**

✔ Check
Did I complete yesterday's tasks?

What will I do today in order to get closer to my goal?

⬚
⬚
⬚

⟦⟧ **Focus**

Which of my core values do I want to focus on today?

What is important today?

⏱ **Weekly Reflection**

How about meditation?

How consistently have I been working on habits over the last 14 days?

Which habit(s) do I want to work on in the next 7 days?

👁 Mindfulness

I am **grateful and happy** because ...

....

....

....

➕ Inner Strength

I am **proud** because ...

....

....

....

♛ Mindset

Today is going to be **superb** because ...

....

....

....

🎁 Good Deeds

What can I do for myself today?

....

....

What can I do for others today?

....

....

☼ Successes, Pleasures & Opportunities

....

....

....

🧭 Weekly Reflection

How satisfied am I with myself?

....

....

....

What can I do in the next 7 days to be fully satisfied with myself?

....

....

....

I'm working on this goal today

🔥 **Purpose & Motivation**

The more people benefit (even if only indirectly), the better for your motivation!

Who else will benefit when I reach my goal?

🚀 **Power**

What will I do today in order to get closer to my goal?

☐
☐
☐

☑ **Check**
Did I complete yesterday's tasks?

⟦⟧ **Focus**

Which of my core values do I want to focus on today?

What is important today?

🧭 **Weekly Reflection**

What negative thoughts or feelings (fear, envy, anger, etc.) accompanied me?

How can I accept them without letting them take over?

How do I feel today? ● ● ● ● ● ● ●

👁 Mindfulness

I am **grateful and happy** because ...

....

....

....

➕ Inner Strength

I am **determined** because ...

....

....

....

👑 Mindset

Today is going to be **meaningful** because ...

....

....

....

🎁 Good Deeds

What can I do for myself today?

....

....

What can I do for others today?

....

....

☀ Successes, Pleasures & Opportunities

....

....

....

This can also help: Put your cell phone in airplane mode! ....

🕐 Weekly Reflection

How much time have I spent on unnecessary distractions?

....

....

....

How can I avoid these distractions?

....

....

....

I'm working on this goal today ◎

How will I reward
myself when
I have reached
my goal?

🚀 **Power**

✅ **Check**
Did I complete
yesterday's tasks?

What will I do
today in order
to get closer
to my goal?

☐

☐

☐

⟦⟧ **Focus**

Which of my core values do I want
to focus on today?

What is important today?

⚡ **Weekly Reflection**

What stressed or annoyed me?

How can I avoid or improve this?

👁 Mindfulness

I am **grateful and happy** because ...

⊕ Inner Strength

I am **persevering** because ...

♛ Mindset

Today is going to be **brilliant** because ...

🎁 Good Deeds

What can I do for myself today?

What can I do for others today?

☼ Successes, Pleasures & Opportunities

🧭 Weekly Reflection

How often have I actually done the tasks I have planned?

How can I improve?

I'm working on this goal today

🔥 **Purpose & Motivation**

...... Think again and again about these!

What are the consequences if I don't reach my goal?

🚀 **Power**

✅ **Check**
Did I complete yesterday's tasks?

What will I do today in order to get closer to my goal?

☐
☐
☐

⌗ **Focus**

Which of my core values do I want to focus on today?

What is important today?

🧭 **Weekly Reflection**

What have I done for my own development?

What can I do for my development in the next 7 days?

How do I feel today?   ● ● ● ● ● ● ●

👁 Mindfulness

I am **grateful and happy** because ...

....

....

....

♟ Inner Strength

I am **optimistic** because ...

....

....

....

♛ Mindset

Today is going to be **really good** because ...

....

....

🎁 Good Deeds

What can I do for myself today?

....

....

What can I do for others today?

....

....

☀ Successes, Pleasures & Opportunities

....

....

....

🧭 Weekly Reflection

In which situations have I behaved unfavorably?

....

....

....

What should I do instead?

....

....

....

KEEP
YOUR
FOCUS

> If a man knows not to which port he sails, no wind is favorable.
>
> — Lucius Annaeus Seneca

I'm working on this goal today

🔥 **Purpose & Motivation**

Why do I want to reach this goal?

🚀 **Power**

✅ **Check**
Did I complete yesterday's tasks?

What will I do today in order to get closer to my goal?

⌴ **Focus**

Which of my core values do I want to focus on today?

What is important today?

🧭 **Weekly Reflection**

What robbed me of energy or did me no good?

How can I improve this?

👁 Mindfulness

I am **grateful and happy** because ...

....

....

....

👑 Mindset

Today is going to be **wonderful** because ...

....

....

➕ Inner Strength

I am **successful** because ...

....

....

....

You can only be successful, not become successful!

🎁 Good Deeds

What can I do for myself today?

....

....

What can I do for others today?

....

....

☀ Successes, Pleasures & Opportunities

....

....

....

ⓘ Weekly Reflection

What self-critical beliefs did I notice?

....

....

....

What positive beliefs will I replace them with?

....

....

....

📅 **Day** »

I'm working on this goal today ◎

🔥 **Purpose & Motivation**

Who or what can support me on the way to my goal?

🚀 **Power**

What will I do today in order to get closer to my goal?

☑ **Check**
Did I complete yesterday's tasks?

☐
☐
☐

⟦⟧ **Focus**

Which of my core values do I want to focus on today?

What is important today?

Don't neglect this!

🧭 **Weekly Reflection**

❝❞ Challenge: Did I actually do the tasks I planned and how did it feel?

❝❞ Challenge: What new or unusual actions am I going to take in the next 7 days?

How do I feel today?   ● ● ● ● ● ● ● ☺

👁 Mindfulness

I am **grateful and happy** because …

....

....

....

➕ Inner Strength

I am **competent** because …

....

....

....

👑 Mindset

Today is going to be **excellent** because …

....

....

🎁 Good Deeds

What can I do for myself today?

....

....

What can I do for others today?

....

....

☀ Successes, Pleasures & Opportunities

....

....

....

🧭 Weekly Reflection

How well did I take care of myself?

....

....

....

Do I need to make any improvements?

....

....

....

I'm working on this goal today

🔥 **Purpose & Motivation**

What is going to be better when I have reached my goal?

🚀 **Power**

What will I do today in order to get closer to my goal?

☐
☐
☐

✅ **Check**
Did I complete yesterday's tasks?

⟦⟧ **Focus**

Which of my core values do I want to focus on today?

What is important today?

🧭 **Weekly Reflection**

What was particularly good or gave me pleasure?

How can I cultivate this even more in my life?

👁 Mindfulness

I am **grateful and happy** because …

⊕ Inner Strength

I am **strong** because …

♛ Mindset

Today is going to be **very special** because …

🎁 Good Deeds

What can I do for myself today?

What can I do for others today?

☀ Successes, Pleasures & Opportunities

🕐 Weekly Reflection

When have I felt like a victim or blamed others?

How am I going to handle this better?

I'm working on this goal today

◎

🔥 Purpose & Motivation

How will I feel when I have reached my goal?

🚀 Power

What will I do today in order to get closer to my goal?

☐

☐

☐

✅ Check
Did I complete yesterday's tasks?

🎯 Focus

Which of my core values do I want to focus on today?

What is important today?

🧭 Weekly Reflection

Do you eat healthy?

How consistently have I worked on habit(s) in the last 7 days?

Which habit(s) do I want to work on in the next 7 days?

How do I feel today?   ● ● ● ● ● ● ●

👁 Mindfulness

I am **grateful and happy** because ...

....

....

....

➕ Inner Strength

I am **proud** because ...

....

....

....

👑 Mindset

Today is going to be **superb** because ...

....

....

🎁 Good Deeds

What can I do for myself today?

....

....

What can I do for others today?

....

....

☀ Successes, Pleasures & Opportunities

....

....

....

🕗 Weekly Reflection

How satisfied am I with myself?

....

....

....

What can I do in the next 7 days to be fully satisfied with myself?

....

....

....

I'm working on this goal today

🔥 **Purpose & Motivation**

Who else will benefit when I reach my goal?

🚀 **Power**

What will I do today in order to get closer to my goal?

☑️ **Check**
Did I complete yesterday's tasks?

☐

☐

☐

⟦⟧ **Focus**

Which of my core values do I want to focus on today?

What is important today?

🕐 **Weekly Reflection**

What negative thoughts or feelings (fear, envy, anger, etc.) accompanied me?

How can I accept them without letting them take over?

👁 Mindfulness

I am **grateful and happy** because ...

....

....

....

➕ Inner Strength

I am **determined** because ...

....

....

....

👑 Mindset

Today is going to be **meaningful** because ...

....

....

🎁 Good Deeds

What can I do for myself today?

....

....

What can I do for others today?

....

....

☀ Successes, Pleasures & Opportunities

....

....

....

🧭 Weekly Reflection

How much time have I spent on unnecessary distractions?

....

....

....

How can I avoid these distractions?

....

....

....

I'm working on this goal today ◎ ....
....
....

🔥 **Purpose & Motivation**

How will I reward myself when I have reached my goal? ....
....
....
....

🚀 **Power**

What will I do today in order to get closer to my goal?

☐ ....
☐ ....
☐ ....

✅ **Check**
Did I complete yesterday's tasks?

⌜⌟ **Focus**

Which of my core values do I want to focus on today?
....
....

What is important today?
....
....
....

🧭 **Weekly Reflection**

What stressed or annoyed me?
....
....
....

How can I avoid or improve this?
....
....
....

👁 Mindfulness

I am **grateful and happy** because ...

➕ Inner Strength

I am **persevering** because ...

👑 Mindset

Today is going to be **brilliant** because ...

🎁 Good Deeds

What can I do for myself today?

What can I do for others today?

☀ Successes, Pleasures & Opportunities

⚡ Weekly Reflection

How often have I actually done the tasks I have planned?

How can I improve?

📅 **Day** »

I'm working on this goal today
◎

🔥 **Purpose & Motivation**

What are the consequences if I don't reach my goal?

🚀 **Power**

✅ **Check**
Did I complete yesterday's tasks?

What will I do today in order to get closer to my goal?

☐
☐
☐

⌨ **Focus**

Which of my core values do I want to focus on today?

What is important today?

🧭 **Weekly Reflection**

What have I done for my own development?

What can I do for my development in the next 7 days?

👁 Mindfulness

I am **grateful and happy** because ...

....

....

....

➕ Inner Strength

I am **optimistic** because ...

....

....

....

What would the future version of yourself write? Would you like to try that?

👑 Mindset

Today is going to be **really good** because ...

....

....

🎁 Good Deeds

What can I do for myself today?

....

....

What can I do for others today?

....

....

☀ Successes, Pleasures & Opportunities

....

....

....

🧭 Weekly Reflection

In which situations have I behaved unfavorably?

....

....

....

What should I do instead?

....

....

....

YOU CAN ONLY

» BE «

HAPPY
SUCCESSFUL
FULFILLED
SATISFIED

> Most of the shadows of this life are caused by standing in one's own sunshine.

— Ralph Waldo Emerson

I'm working on this goal today

🔥 **Purpose & Motivation**

Why do I want to reach this goal?

🚀 **Power**

What will I do today in order to get closer to my goal?

☐
☐
☐

✅ **Check**
Did I complete yesterday's tasks?

⌞⌝ **Focus**

Which of my core values do I want to focus on today?

What is important today?

⚡ **Weekly Reflection**

What robbed me of energy or did me no good?

How can I improve this?

👁 Mindfulness

I am **grateful and happy** because ...

....

....

....

➕ Inner Strength

I am **successful** because ...

....

....

....

👑 Mindset

Today is going to be **wonderful** because ...

....

....

🎁 Good Deeds

What can I do for myself today?

....

....

What can I do for others today?

....

....

☀ Successes, Pleasures & Opportunities

....

....

....

... *What you believe determines your life!* ...

🧭 Weekly Reflection

What self-critical beliefs did I notice?

....

....

....

What positive beliefs will I replace them with?

....

....

....

I'm working on this goal today ⊚

🔥 **Purpose & Motivation**

Who or what can support me on the way to my goal?

🚀 **Power**

What will I do today in order to get closer to my goal?

☐
☐
☐

✅ **Check**
Did I complete yesterday's tasks?

⌜⌟ **Focus**

Which of my core values do I want to focus on today?

What is important today?

🕐 **Weekly Reflection**

❝❝ Challenge: Did I actually do the tasks I planned and how did it feel?

❝❝ Challenge: What new or unusual actions am I going to take in the next 7 days?

👁 Mindfulness

I am **grateful and happy** because ...

....

....

....

➕ Inner Strength

I am **competent** because ...

....

....

....

👑 Mindset

Today is going to be **excellent** because ...

....

....

....

🎁 Good Deeds

What can I do for myself today?

....

....

What can I do for others today?

....

....

☀ Successes, Pleasures & Opportunities

....

....

....

Have you tried going to the gym? ....

🧭 Weekly Reflection

How well did I take care of myself?

....

....

....

Do I need to make any improvements?

....

....

....

I'm working on this goal today

🔥 **Purpose & Motivation**

What is going to be better when I have reached my goal?

🚀 **Power**

What will I do today in order to get closer to my goal?

☐
☐
☐

✅ **Check**
Did I complete yesterday's tasks?

⟦⟧ **Focus**

Which of my core values do I want to focus on today?

What is important today?

🧭 **Weekly Reflection**

What was particularly good or gave me pleasure?

How can I cultivate this even more in my life?

How do I feel today? ● ● ● ● ● ● ●

👁 Mindfulness

I am **grateful and happy** because ...

_____

_____

_____

➕ Inner Strength

I am **strong** because ...

_____

_____

_____

♛ Mindset

Today is going to be **very special** because ...

_____

_____

🎁 Good Deeds

What can I do for myself today?

_____

_____

What can I do for others today?

_____

_____

☀ Successes, Pleasures & Opportunities

_____

_____

_____

🕐 Weekly Reflection

When have I felt like a victim or blamed others?

_____

_____

_____

How am I going to handle this better?

_____

_____

_____

📅 Day »

75

I'm working on this goal today

🔥 Purpose & Motivation

How will I feel when I have reached my goal?

🚀 Power

What will I do today in order to get closer to my goal?

✅ Check
Did I complete yesterday's tasks?

☐
☐
☐

⟦ ⟧ Focus

Which of my core values do I want to focus on today?

What is important today?

⚡ Weekly Reflection

How consistently have I worked on habit(s) in the last 7 days?

Which habit(s) do I want to work on in the next 7 days?

220

How do I feel today? ☹ ● ● ● ● ● ● ● ☺

👁 Mindfulness

I am **grateful and happy** because ...

....

....

....

♛ Mindset

Today is going to be **superb** because ...

....

....

🎁 Good Deeds

What can I do for myself today?

....

....

☀ Successes, Pleasures & Opportunities

....

....

....

⚡ Inner Strength

I am **proud** because ...

....

....

....

What can I do for others today?

....

....

🧭 Weekly Reflection

How satisfied am I with myself?

....

....

....

What can I do in the next 7 days to be fully satisfied with myself?

....

....

....

I'm working on this goal today

🔥 **Purpose & Motivation**

Who else will benefit when I reach my goal?

🚀 **Power**

What will I do today in order to get closer to my goal?

☐

☐

☐

✅ **Check**
Did I complete yesterday's tasks?

⌌⌍ **Focus**

Which of my core values do I want to focus on today?

What is important today?

Have you internalized your power questions (see page 31)?

🧭 **Weekly Reflection**

What negative thoughts or feelings (fear, envy, anger, etc.) accompanied me?

How can I accept them without letting them take over?

👁 Mindfulness

I am **grateful and happy** because …

➕ Inner Strength

I am **determined** because …

👑 Mindset

Today is going to be **meaningful** because …

🎁 Good Deeds

What can I do for myself today?

What can I do for others today?

☀ Successes, Pleasures & Opportunities

🧭 Weekly Reflection

How much time have I spent on unnecessary distractions?

How can I avoid these distractions?

I'm working on this goal today

🔥 **Purpose & Motivation**

How will I reward myself when I have reached my goal?

🚀 **Power**

What will I do today in order to get closer to my goal?

☑ **Check**
Did I complete yesterday's tasks?

⟦ ⟧ **Focus**

Which of my core values do I want to focus on today?

What is important today?

🕐 **Weekly Reflection**

What stressed or annoyed me?

How can I avoid or improve this?

How do I feel today? ☹ ● ● ● ● ● ● ● ☺

👁 Mindfulness

I am **grateful and happy** because ...

➕ Inner Strength

I am **persevering** because ...

♛ Mindset

Today is going to be **brilliant** because ...

🎁 Good Deeds

What can I do for myself today?

What can I do for others today?

☀ Successes, Pleasures & Opportunities

Weekly Reflection

How often have I actually done the tasks
I have planned?

How can I improve?

🎯 I'm working on this goal today

🔥 **Purpose & Motivation**

What are the consequences if I don't reach my goal?

🚀 **Power**

What will I do today in order to get closer to my goal?

☐
☐
☐

Don't forget! ⋯⋯⋯►

✅ **Check**
Did I complete yesterday's tasks?

⟦ ⟧ **Focus**

Which of my core values do I want to focus on today?

What is important today?

🌀 **Weekly Reflection**

What have I done for my own development?

What can I do for my development in the next 7 days?

How do I feel today? ☹ ● ● ● ● ● ● ● ☺

👁 Mindfulness

I am **grateful and happy** because ...

....

....

....

➕ Inner Strength

I am **optimistic** because ...

....

....

....

♛ Mindset

Today is going to be **really good** because ...

....

....

🎁 Good Deeds

What can I do for myself today?

....

....

What can I do for others today?

....

....

☼ Successes, Pleasures & Opportunities

....

....

....

🧭 Weekly Reflection

In which situations have I behaved unfavorably?

....

....

....

What should I do instead?

....

....

....

→ EVERY ←

DAY

IS A

NEW

CHANCE

> It is not because things are difficult that we do not dare;
> it is because we do not dare that they are difficult.
>
> — Lucius Annaeus Seneca

I'm working on this goal today ◎

🔥 **Purpose & Motivation**

Why do I want to reach this goal?

🚀 **Power**

What will I do today in order to get closer to my goal?

☐
☐
☐

✅ **Check**
Did I complete yesterday's tasks?

⟦ ⟧ **Focus**

Which of my core values do I want to focus on today?

What is important today?

⏱ **Weekly Reflection**

What robbed me of energy or did me no good?

How can I improve this?

👁 Mindfulness

I am **grateful and happy** because ...

....

....

....

➕ Inner Strength

I am **successful** because ...

....

....

....

♛ Mindset

Today is going to be **wonderful** because ...

....

....

....

🎁 Good Deeds

What can I do for myself today?

....

....

What can I do for others today?

....

....

☀ Successes, Pleasures & Opportunities

....

....

....

🧭 Weekly Reflection

What self-critical beliefs did I notice?

....

....

....

What positive beliefs will I replace them with?

....

....

....

I'm working on this goal today

🔥 **Purpose & Motivation**

Who or what can support me on the way to my goal?

🚀 **Power**

What will I do today in order to get closer to my goal?

☑ **Check**
Did I complete yesterday's tasks?

⚙ **Focus**

Which of my core values do I want to focus on today?

What is important today?

🕐 **Weekly Reflection**

❝❝ Challenge: Did I actually do the tasks I planned and how did it feel?

❝❝ Challenge: What new or unusual actions am I going to take in the next weeks?

How do I feel today? ● ● ● ● ● ● ●

👁 Mindfulness

I am **grateful and happy** because ...

⊕ Inner Strength

I am **competent** because ...

♛ Mindset

Today is going to be **excellent** because ...

🎁 Good Deeds

What can I do for myself today?

What can I do for others today?

☀ Successes, Pleasures & Opportunities

⊘ Weekly Reflection

How well did I take care of myself?

Do I need to make any improvements?

I'm working on this goal today ◎

What is going to
be better when
I have reached
my goal?

🚀 **Power**

☑ **Check**
Did I complete
yesterday's tasks?

What will I do
today in order
to get closer
to my goal?

☐

☐

☐

⌗ **Focus**

Which of my core values do I want
to focus on today?

What is important today?

🧭 **Weekly Reflection**

What was particularly good or gave me
pleasure?

How can I cultivate this even more in
my life?

👁 Mindfulness

I am **grateful and happy** because ...

....

....

....

➕ Inner Strength

I am **strong** because ...

....

....

....

👑 Mindset

Today is going to be **very special** because ...

....

....

🎁 Good Deeds

What can I do for myself today?

....

....

What can I do for others today?

....

....

☀ Successes, Pleasures & Opportunities

....

....

....

🧭 Weekly Reflection

When have I felt like a victim or blamed others?

....

....

....

How am I going to handle this better?

....

....

....

I'm working on this goal today 🎯

🔥 **Purpose & Motivation**

How will I feel when I have reached my goal?

🚀 **Power**

What will I do today in order to get closer to my goal?

☐
☐
☐

✅ **Check**
Did I complete yesterday's tasks?

⟦⟧ **Focus**

Which of my core values do I want to focus on today?

What is important today?

🧭 **Weekly Reflection**

How consistently have I worked on habit(s) in the last 7 days?

Which habit(s) do I want to focus on in the next weeks?

How do I feel today?   ○ ○ ○ ○ ○ ○ ○ ☺

👁 Mindfulness

I am **grateful and happy** because ...

....

....

....

♛ Inner Strength

I am **proud** because ...

....

....

....

♛ Mindset

Today is going to be **superb** because ...

....

....

🎁 Good Deeds

What can I do for myself today?

....

....

What can I do for others today?

....

....

☀ Successes, Pleasures & Opportunities

....

....

....

🧭 Weekly Reflection

How satisfied am I with myself?

....

....

....

What can I do in the next weeks to be as satisfied with myself as possible?

....

....

....

I'm working on this goal today ◎

🔥 **Purpose & Motivation**

Who else will benefit when I reach my goal?

🚀 **Power**

What will I do today in order to get closer to my goal?

☐
☐
☐

✅ **Check**
Did I complete yesterday's tasks?

[] **Focus**

Which of my core values do I want to focus on today?

What is important today?

🧭 **Weekly Reflection**

What negative thoughts or feelings (fear, envy, anger, etc.) accompanied me?

How can I accept them without letting them take over?

How do I feel today? ● ● ● ● ● ●

👁 Mindfulness

I am **grateful and happy** because ...

➕ Inner Strength

I am **determined** because ...

👑 Mindset

Today is going to be **meaningful** because ...

🎁 Good Deeds

What can I do for myself today?

What can I do for others today?

☀ Successes, Pleasures & Opportunities

Energy flows where attention goes!

🕐 Weekly Reflection

How much time have I spent on unnecessary distractions?

How can I avoid these distractions?

I'm working on this goal today

🔥 **Purpose & Motivation**

How will I reward myself when I have reached my goal?

🚀 **Power**

What will I do today in order to get closer to my goal?

☐
☐
☐

✅ **Check**
Did I complete yesterday's tasks?

⬚ **Focus**

Which of my core values do I want to focus on today?

What is important today?

🧭 **Weekly Reflection**

What stressed or annoyed me?

How can I avoid or improve this?

👁 Mindfulness

I am **grateful and happy** because …

....

....

....

👑 Mindset

Today is going to be **brilliant** because …

....

....

🎁 Good Deeds

What can I do for myself today?

....

....

⊕ Inner Strength

I am **persevering** because …

....

....

....

What can I do for others today?

....

....

☼ Successes, Pleasures & Opportunities

....

....

....

🧭 Weekly Reflection

How often have I actually done the tasks
I have planned?

....

....

....

How can I improve?

....

....

....

I'm working on this goal today

◎

🔥 **Purpose & Motivation**

What are the
consequences
if I don't reach
my goal?

🚀 **Power**

What will I do
today in order
to get closer
to my goal?

☐
☐
☐

✅ **Check**
Did I complete
yesterday's tasks?

⟦⟧ **Focus**

Which of my core values do I want
to focus on today?

What is important today?

✒ **Weekly Reflection**

What have I done for my own
development?

What can I do for my personal
development in the next weeks?

How do I feel today?

👁 Mindfulness

I am **grateful and happy** because ...

➕ Inner Strength

I am **optimistic** because ...

♛ Mindset

Today is going to be **really good** because ...

🎁 Good Deeds

What can I do for myself today?

What can I do for others today?

☀ Successes, Pleasures & Opportunities

ⓩ Weekly Reflection

In which situations have I behaved unfavorably?

What should I do instead?

↑

FOLLOW YOUR VISION

❝ He who knows all the answers has not been asked all the questions.

— Confucius

📅 **Day** »

I'm working on this goal today

🔥 **Purpose & Motivation**

Why do I want to reach this goal?

🚀 **Power**

What will I do today in order to get closer to my goal?

☐
☐
☐

☑️ **Check**
Did I complete yesterday's tasks?

⌗ **Focus**

Which of my core values do I want to focus on today?

What is important today?

🕐 **Monthly Reflection**

What do I want most right now?

What will I do to get it?

How do I feel today? ☹ ● ● ● ● ● ● ● ☺

👁 Mindfulness

I am **grateful and happy** because ...

....

....

....

♔ Mindset

Today is going to be **wonderful** because ...

....

....

🎁 Good Deeds

What can I do for myself today?

....

....

What can I do for others today?

....

....

☀ Successes, Pleasures & Opportunities

....

....

....

➕ Inner Strength

I am **successful** because ...

....

....

....

ⓘ Monthly Reflection

How have the last few weeks been?

....

....

....

How do I want the next weeks to be and what do I need to do?

....

....

....

I'm working on this goal today

🔥 **Purpose & Motivation**

Who or what can support me on the way to my goal?

🚀 **Power**

What will I do today in order to get closer to my goal?

☑ **Check**
Did I complete yesterday's tasks?

☐

☐

☐

⌗ **Focus**

Which of my core values do I want to focus on today?

What is important today?

🧭 **Monthly Reflection**

How satisfied am I with my physical condition?

Do I have to change anything? What is it? How can I do it?

How do I feel today?   ☹ ● ● ● ● ● ● ● ☺

👁 Mindfulness

I am **grateful and happy** because ...

....

....

....

♔ Mindset

Today is going to be **excellent** because ...

....

....

➕ Inner Strength

I am **competent** because ...

....

....

....

🎁 Good Deeds

What can I do for myself today?

....

....

What can I do for others today?

....

....

☀ Successes, Pleasures & Opportunities

....

....

....

🧭 Monthly Reflection

How satisfied am I with my mental state?

....

....

....

Do I have to change anything?
What is it? And how can I do it?

....

....

....

I'm working on this goal today

🔥 Purpose & Motivation

What is going to be better when I have reached the goal?

🚀 Power

What will I do today in order to get closer to my goal?

☑ **Check**
Did I complete yesterday's tasks?

⟦ ⟧ Focus

Which of my core values do I want to focus on today?

What is important today?

⏱ Monthly Reflection

How have I incorporated my core values that are important to me?

How can I integrate them even better into my life?

👁 Mindfulness

I am **grateful and happy** because ...

....

....

....

⊕ Inner Strength

I am **strong** because ...

....

....

....

♛ Mindset

Today is going to be **very special** because ...

....

....

🎁 Good Deeds

What can I do for myself today?

....

....

What can I do for others today?

....

....

☀ Successes, Pleasures & Opportunities

....

....

....

🕐 Monthly Reflection

How have I progressed toward my goals?

....

....

....

What do I have to correct or how can I improve?

....

....

....

I'm working on this goal today

🔥 **Purpose & Motivation**

How will I feel when I have reached my goal?

🚀 **Power**

What will I do today in order to get closer to my goal?

☑ **Check**
Did I complete yesterday's tasks?

☐

☐

☐

⟦⟧ **Focus**

Which of my core values do I want to focus on today?

What is important today?

🧭 **Monthly Reflection**

What was I particularly preoccupied with or worried about?

What can I do to change it or better deal with it?

How do I feel today?   ☹ ● ● ● ● ● ● ● ☺

👁 Mindfulness

I am **grateful and happy** because ...

....

....

....

➕ Inner Strength

I am **proud** because ...

....

....

....

👑 Mindset

Today is going to be **superb** because ...

....

....

🎁 Good Deeds

What can I do for myself today?

....

....

What can I do for others today?

....

....

☀ Successes, Pleasures & Opportunities

....

....

....

Monthly Reflection

How much joy, fun, and free time for great experiences were there in the last weeks?

....

....

....

How can I consciously integrate them into my life in the next few weeks?

....

....

....

I'm working on this goal today

◉

🔥 Purpose & Motivation

Who else will profit when I reach my goal?

🚀 Power

What will I do today in order to get closer to my goal?

☐
☐
☐

> ✅ **Check**
> Did I complete yesterday's tasks?

⟦ ⟧ Focus

Which of my core values do I want to focus on today?

What is important today?

🖋 Monthly Reflection

How consistently did I keep focus on the important things?

How can I spend more time with important things?

👁 Mindfulness

I am **grateful and happy** because ...

➕ Inner Strength

I am **determined** because ...

👑 Mindset

Today is going to be **meaningful** because ...

🎁 Good Deeds

What can I do for myself today?

What can I do for others today?

☀ Successes, Pleasures & Opportunities

 Monthly Reflection

Where did I use excuses not to do something I planned to do?

What can I do to improve in the future?

I'm working on this goal today

🔥 **Purpose & Motivation**

How will I reward myself when I have reached my goal?

🚀 **Power**

☑ **Check**
Did I complete yesterday's tasks?

What will I do today in order to get closer to my goal?

☐

☐

☐

⌗ **Focus**

What is important today?

Which of my core values do I want to focus on today?

🧭 **Monthly Reflection**

What was my biggest challenge in the last few weeks?

What could I have done better?

How do I feel today? ● ● ● ● ● ● ●

👁 Mindfulness

I am **grateful and happy** because ...

....

....

....

👑 Mindset

Today is going to be **brilliant** because ...

....

....

🎁 Good Deeds

What can I do for myself today?

....

....

☀ Successes, Pleasures & Opportunities

....

....

....

⊕ Inner Strength

I am **persevering** because ...

....

....

....

What can I do for others today?

....

....

🕐 Monthly Reflection

How satisfied am I with myself and my personal development?

....

....

....

Do I have to change anything? What is it? And how can I do it?

....

....

....

I'm working on this goal today

🔥 Purpose & Motivation

What are the consequences if I don't reach the goal?

🚀 Power

What will I do today in order to get closer to my goal?

☐
☐
☐

✅ Check
Did I complete yesterday's tasks?

⟦ ⟧ Focus

Which of my core values do I want to focus on today?

What is important today?

🧭 Monthly Reflection

In which areas of my life do I currently have shortcomings?

Do I want or have to live with them? What can I do to improve?

👁 Mindfulness

I am **grateful and happy** because ...

....

....

....

➕ Inner Strength

I am **optimistic** because ...

....

....

....

♛ Mindset

Today is going to be **really good** because ...

....

....

🎁 Good Deeds

What can I do for myself today?

....

....

What can I do for others today?

....

....

☀ Successes, Pleasures & Opportunities

....

....

....

🧭 Monthly Reflection

What dreams do I have that I would like to fulfill in the near future?

....

....

....

How and when will I implement them?

....

....

....

10 STEPS IN
1 DIRECTION

—————— NOT ——————

1 STEP IN
10 DIRECTIONS

> It does not matter how slowly you go as long as you do not stop.
>
> — Confucius

📅 Day »

I'm working on this goal today ◎

🔥 Purpose & Motivation

Why do I want
to reach this
goal?

🚀 Power

What will I do
today in order
to get closer
to my goal?

☐

☐

☐

✅ Check
Did I complete
yesterday's tasks?

⛶ Focus

Which of my core values do I want
to focus on today?

What is important today?

*If you have not yet defined a life
vision for yourself, do so now
(see pages 34-35).*

🧭 Quarterly Reflection

What separates me today from the vision
I have of my life?

How well am I on track toward this vision?
Do I have to change anything?

262

👁 Mindfulness

I am **grateful and happy** because ...

....

....

....

➕ Inner Strength

I am **successful** because ...

....

....

....

♛ Mindset

Today is going to be **wonderful** because ...

....

....

🎁 Good Deeds

What can I do for myself today?

....

....

What can I do for others today?

....

....

☀ Successes, Pleasures & Opportunities

....

....

....

🧭 Quarterly Reflection

What have I done for my further education in the last few months?

....

....

....

How do I plan to work on my further education in the coming months?

....

....

....

I'm working on this goal today ◎

🔥 **Purpose & Motivation**

Who or what
can support
me on the way
to my goal?

🚀 **Power**

What will I do
today in order
to get closer
to my goal?

☐
☐
☐

✅ **Check**
Did I complete
yesterday's tasks?

⟦⟧ **Focus**

Which of my core values do I want
to focus on today?

What is important today?

📝 **Quarterly Reflection**

How consistent is my style and my attitude
with the person I want to be?

Can I change anything? What is it?
And how will I do it?

How do I feel today? ⊗ ● ● ● ● ● ● ● ☺

👁 Mindfulness

I am **grateful and happy** because ...

....

....

....

♔ Mindset

Today is going to be **excellent** because ...

....

....

🎁 Good Deeds

What can I do for myself today?

....

....

What can I do for others today?

....

....

☀ Successes, Pleasures & Opportunities

....

....

....

This might feel silly and superficial at first, but it helps. I recommend the book Awaken the Giant Within by Anthony Robbins.

❷ Quarterly Reflection

What words do I often use to express negative feelings?

....

....

....

What words can I say instead to soften these feelings?

....

....

....

I'm working on this goal today

🔥 **Purpose & Motivation**

What is going to be better when I have reached the goal?

🚀 **Power**

What will I do today in order to get closer to my goal?

☐
☐
☐

✅ **Check**
Did I complete yesterday's tasks?

⟦⟧ **Focus**

Which of my core values do I want to focus on today?

What is important today?

Sometimes only self-imposed limits stop you! »»»»»»

⚡ **Quarterly Reflection**

What actions are stopping me from achieving my goals?

How can I still achieve them?

How do I feel today? ● ● ● ● ● ● ●

👁 Mindfulness

I am **grateful and happy** because ...

....

....

....

➕ Inner Strength

I am **strong** because ...

....

....

....

👑 Mindset

Today is going to be **very special** because ...

....

....

🎁 Good Deeds

What can I do for myself today?

....

....

What can I do for others today?

....

....

☀ Successes, Pleasures & Opportunities

....

....

....

⚫ Quarterly Reflection

How happy am I with my home and surroundings?

....

....

....

What do I want to change in the near future in order to feel great all around?

....

....

....

I'm working on this goal today ◎ ....
....
....

🔥 Purpose & Motivation

How will I feel when I have reached my goal?
....
....
....
....

🚀 Power

What will I do today in order to get closer to my goal?

☐ ....
☐ ....
☐ ....

☑ Check
Did I complete yesterday's tasks?

⟦ ⟧ Focus

Which of my core values do I want to focus on today?
....
....

What is important today?
....
....
....

🧭 Quarterly Reflection

Which five people have I spent the most time with, real or imaginary?
....
....
....

How well do they fit into my vision and my goals? Should I change anything?
....
....
....

👁 **Mindfulness**

I am **grateful and happy** because …

....

....

....

⊕ **Inner Strength**

I am **proud** because …

....

....

....

How many times have you checked here?

♛ **Mindset**

Today is going to be **superb** because …

....

....

....

🎁 **Good Deeds**

What can I do for myself today?

....

....

What can I do for others today?

....

....

☼ **Successes, Pleasures & Opportunities**

....

....

....

....

◉ **Quarterly Reflection**

How good does my daily routine feel?

....

....

....

What can I improve to make my day feel perfect?

....

....

....

I'm working on this goal today 🎯

🔥 **Purpose & Motivation**

Who else will profit when I reach my goal?

🚀 **Power**

What will I do today in order to get closer to my goal?

☐
☐
☐

✅ **Check**
Did I complete yesterday's tasks?

⌗ **Focus**

Which of my core values do I want to focus on today?

What is important today?

🌀 **Quarterly Reflection**

How satisfied am I with my relationships?

What can I do to make them better in the near future?

👁 Mindfulness

I am **grateful and happy** because …

....

....

....

♛ Mindset

Today is going to be **meaningful** because …

....

....

🎁 Good Deeds

What can I do for myself today?

....

....

⊕ Inner Strength

I am **determined** because …

....

....

....

What can I do for others today?

....

....

☀ Successes, Pleasures & Opportunities

....

....

....

Be courageous and speak to these people!

❶ Quarterly Reflection

Which teachers, mentors, supporters, or companions do I have in my life?

....

....

....

Who else can teach me and help me develop?

....

....

....

I'm working
on this goal
today

🔥 **Purpose & Motivation**

How will I reward
myself when
I have reached
my goal?

🚀 **Power**

☑ **Check**
Did I complete
yesterday's tasks?

What will I do
today in order
to get closer
to my goal?

☐

☐

☐

⌗ **Focus**

What is important today?

Which of my core values do I want
to focus on today?

🧭 **Quarterly Reflection**

How satisfied am I with my financial
situation?

What do I need to improve my financial
status?

How do I feel today?   ● ● ● ● ● ● ●

👁 Mindfulness

I am **grateful and happy** because …

....

....

....

👑 Mindset

Today is going to be **brilliant** because …

....

....

🎁 Good Deeds

What can I do for myself today?

....

....

☀ Successes, Pleasures & Opportunities

....

....

....

➕ Inner Strength

I am **persevering** because …

....

....

....

What can I do for others today?

....

....

The longer you put something off, the harder it gets!

🕐 Quarterly Reflection

What's bothering me because I'm avoiding it or keep pushing it aside?

....

....

....

What can I do to deal with this?

....

....

....

I'm working on this goal today

🔥 Purpose & Motivation

What are the consequences if I don't reach the goal?

🚀 Power

What will I do today in order to get closer to my goal?

☐

☐

☐

✅ **Check**
Did I complete yesterday's tasks?

[ ] Focus

Which of my core values do I want to focus on today?

What is important today?

🧭 Quarterly Reflection

Which people do I particularly admire at the moment? Why?

What can I learn from them?

👁 Mindfulness

I am **grateful and happy** because ...

....

....

....

♟ Mindset

Today is going to be **really good** because ...

....

....

🎁 Good Deeds

What can I do for myself today?

....

....

☀ Successes, Pleasures & Opportunities

....

....

....

✚ Inner Strength

I am **optimistic** because ...

....

....

....

What can I do for others today?

....

....

See the advice on page 265.

❼ Quarterly Reflection

What words do I often use to express positive feelings?

....

....

....

What words could I use instead to amplify these feelings?

....

....

....

I'm working on this goal today

🔥 Purpose & Motivation

Why do I want to reach this goal?

🚀 Power

What will I do today in order to get closer to my goal?

☐
☐
☐

✅ **Check**
Did I complete yesterday's tasks?

⌷ Focus

Which of my core values do I want to focus on today?

What is important today?

Where are you now compared to when you started? Check your wheel of life (see page 36).

🕐 Final Reflection

How well have I used these 100 days for my personal growth and to reach my goals?

What could I have done better?

How do I feel today? ● ● ● ● ● ● ●

👁 Mindfulness

I am **grateful and happy** because ...

_____

_____

_____

♔ Mindset

Der Tag wird heute **wundervoll**, weil ...

_____

_____

🎁 Good Deeds

What can I do for myself today?

_____

_____

⊕ Inner Strength

I am **successful** because ...

_____

_____

_____

Congratulations, you've worked on yourself and your goals for 100 days! Well done!

What can I do for others today?

_____

_____

☀ Successes, Pleasures & Opportunities

_____

_____

_____

No matter how you do it, please keep going and stay on your path!

🧭 Final Reflection

How clearly do I have my next goals and life vision in mind?

_____

_____

_____

How do I want to proceed?

_____

_____

_____

277

My Goal Evaluation

Did you achieve your goals? If so, congratulations! Celebrate and reward yourself! If you missed your goal, don't worry and beat yourself up. After some reflection you will realize that you gained beneficial insight to get even better results for the next time.

You have gained a lot of experience on the way to your goal, and your are fully equipped to draw valuable conclusions for your future, which will make you stronger and more successful. Be sure to write them down below.

Draw how well you've hit your goal.

Goal 1:

How well did I reach my goal?

What experiences did I gain?

What is the consequence? Reward or punishment? When do I put this into action?

Goal 2:

How well did I reach my goal?

What experiences did I gain?

What is the consequence? Reward or punishment? When do I put this into action?

> *Difficulties strengthen the mind, as labor does the body.*
>
> — Lucius Annaeus Seneca

Goal 3:

How well did I reach
my goal?

- - - - - - - - - - - - - ->

What experiences
did I gain?

What is the consequence? Reward or punishment? When do I put this into action?

📅

Goal 4:

How well did I reach
my goal?

- - - - - - - - - - - - - ->

What experiences
did I gain?

What is the consequence? Reward or punishment? When do I put this into action?

📅

Goal 5:

How well did I reach
my goal?

- - - - - - - - - - - - - ->

What experiences
did I gain?

What is the consequence? Reward or punishment? When do I put this into action?

📅

Remarkable Successes

HIGHLIGHTS & GREAT MOMENTS

★
★
★
★
★
★
★
★
★
★
★
★
★
★
★
★
★
★
★

Write down the big points and all the remarkable things you achieved or experienced.